Buyer Personas

How to Gain Insight into Your Customer's Expectations, Align Your Marketing Strategies, and Win More Business

Adele Revella

WILEY

This book is dedicated to every marketer who questions the wisdom of making stuff up.

Contents

Foreword   David Meerman Scott   *xiii*

Acknowledgments   *xvii*

Introduction: Listen First, Then Speak   *xix*

    Why Is Everyone Talking about Buyer Personas?   *xx*

    Will This Approach Work for You?   *xxii*

PART I   **Understanding the Art and Science of**
            Buyer Personas   **1**

Chapter 1   Understand Buying Decisions and the People Who
            Make Them   **3**

    Why the "Know Your Customer" Rule Has Been
      Redefined   *5*

    A Clothes Dryer's Extra Setting Made All the Difference   *6*

    Will You Understand Your Buyers' Decisions?   *7*

    Relying on Buyer Demographics and Psychographics   *10*

    How Marketers Benefit from Buyer Profiles   *11*

    Buying Insights Complete Your Persona   *12*

    High-Consideration Decisions Reveal the
      Best Insights   *13*

    Buying Insights from a Quick Trip to London   *15*

Chapter 2   Focus on the Insights That Guide Marketing
                Decisions   19
                Listening to Kathy   20
                Frustrated, A Newly Minted Consultant
                   Invents Personas   22
                Buyers Have Distinct Expectations   23
                The 5 Rings of Buying Insight   25
                Give Your Buyer a Seat at the Table   27
                Buying Insight Opens Doors to C-Level Executives   31

Chapter 3   Decide How You Will Discover Buyer
                Persona Insights   35
                The Most Important Nine Months of My Career   36
                How Interviews Reveal Insight   38
                Is This Another Kind of Qualitative Research?   39
                Crafting The Low-Consideration Buyer's Story   41
                Using B2B Salespeople to Build Buyer Personas   42
                The Pros and Cons of Buyer Surveys   43
                When to Use Focus Groups   44
                Will Big Data Deliver Insights?   45
                How Social Media Contributes to Buyer Personas   48
                SAP Gains High-Value Insights through Web Analytics 49

PART II   **Interviewing for Buying Insights**   **51**

Chapter 4   Gain Permission and Schedule Buyer Interviews   55
                Persuade Stakeholders That You Need Buying Insights 56
                Overcome the "We Know Our Buyers" Objection   57
                When You Don't Have Time for Buyer
                   Persona Interviews   59
                Use Your Sales Database to Find Buyers to Interview 60

Sometimes You Want to Avoid Your Internal Database   61

*Using Professional Recruiters to Set Interview
   Appointments*   62

Which Buyer Should You Interview?   64

*Interview Buyers Who Chose You as Well
   as Those Who Did Not*   66

Contacting Buyers to Request an Interview   68

Chapter 5   Conduct Probing Buyer Interviews   73

Who Should Conduct the Interview?   74

Prepare for Your Buyer Interview   75

Getting It on the Record   77

"Take Me Back to the Day . . ."   78

Use Your Buyer's Words to Probe for Insight   80

Go Slowly to Capture the Whole Story   81

Questions That Keep the Conversation Flowing   82

An Example Interview with Tim   84

Look for Insight When Buyers Use Jargon   86

Make Your Questions about Your Impact Count   88

Probing on Who Influences This Decision   90

*Asking about the Perceived Value of Your
   Differentiators*   91

When Features Affect Decisions, Look for Insight   92

First and Foremost, Be a Respectful Listener   94

Chapter 6   Mine Your Interviews for Buying Insights   97

You Need Fewer Interviews Than You Expect   98

Step 1: Mark Up Your Interview Transcript   99

Step 2: Organize the Story Based on Buying Insights   103

Step 3: Write a Headline for Each Key Insight   106

Chapter 7 Determine How Many Buyer Personas You Need 111

Segment Buyers Based on Insights, Not Profiles 112

Conduct More Interviews to Test Segmentation Options 114

Analyze Insights to Decide How Many Personas 117

*Will Two Buyer Personas Help You Win
    More Business?* 118

Presenting Your Buyer Persona 123

Copywriting Your Buying Insights 127

Building the Buyer Profile 128

How to Find Buyer Profile Information 129

PART III **Aligning Your Strategies to Win More
Business** **131**

Chapter 8 Decide What to Say to Buyers 135

Will Your Current Approach Work? 136

Set the Agenda, and Invite the Right People 138

Ask for Premeeting Contributions 139

Develop a Complete List of Capabilities That Matter 140

The Moderator Is a Proxy for the Buyer 142

Apply Two Filters for Short Messaging 143

Evaluate Your Competitive Ranking 144

Assess Relative Value to Buyers 145

Bring in the Copywriters and Creative Teams 150

Chapter 9 Design Marketing Activities to Enable Your Buyer's
Journey 151

Understand the Buyer's Journey 153

Patrick's Journey for an Employee Benefits Decision 154

Prioritize Assets That Align with the Buyer's Journey 156

Prepare to Be Surprised 157

How Buyer Personas Affect Industry or Solution
  Marketing   158
A Global Perspective on Buyer Personas and Campaigns 160
Can You Be Useful to People Who Aren't Buying?   162
Educate Buyers That Success Is within Reach   163
Autodesk Helps Buyers Achieve Their Top Priorities   164

Chapter 10   Align Sales and Marketing to Help Buyers Decide   171
Changing the Conversation with Salespeople   173
Share Insights, Not Buyer Personas   174
Deliver Buying Insights through Sales Playbooks   175
Enabling the Challenger Sale   176
Helping Salespeople Break into the C-Suite   177
Insight into the Nurse's Emotions Halts Sales Losses   179
Sales and Marketing: Vive La Différence!   183

Chapter 11   Start Small, with an Eye to the Future   185
Where to Begin Your Buyer Persona Initiative   186
How to Earn Your Stripes as a Strategic Resource   188
How Buyer Personas Benefit Product Strategy   190
Building Buyer Personas for New Products   192
Communicating Insights That Affect Other Teams   193
Using Buyer Personas to Guide Strategic Planning   194
Start Small and Make a Big Difference   198

Bibliography   199
Index   203

Foreword

Back in 2007, I gushed enthusiastically on my blog about the GoPro digital camera, which I had purchased to take photos and videos while surfing. I was a very early adopter (the digital version had been out only a month).

The clever marketers at GoPro focused on creating cameras that address the specific problems faced by consumers, in my case a camera I could take surfing. Not long after my original post, I interviewed Nick Woodman, Founder and Chief Executive Officer (CEO) of GoPro, who told me how his company makes decisions. "Our solutions could never evolve from a boardroom discussion," he told me. "We go straight to the source. We don't ask our grandmother what she thinks about our motorsport mounts apparatus; we ask race car drivers."

Although he didn't call what he was doing buyer persona research, Nick leads a company that builds product and marketing strategies using the ideas that you'll read about in these pages.

So how is GoPro doing now, seven years after the first digital camera was launched and I first wrote about the company? Sales have doubled every year, with the company reporting $279 million in revenue for the three months ending September 30, 2014. This rapid growth allowed GoPro to go public on the stock market in 2014. From zero revenue to a billion dollars a year in less than a decade! As I write this, the company has a market capitalization of $10 billion, making Nick a billionaire. GoPro has left its competitors in the dust through an intense focus on understanding their buyers' expectations!

In this book you will learn how to gain insights into your buyer's mind-set so that you can create and market what your buyers are seeking. You'll see how to differentiate the needs of distinct groups of buyers—in the case of GoPro not just digital camera buyers but surfers, race car drivers, and skydivers—in buyer personas that guide your company to breakthrough success.

This approach is utterly different from most companies. Either they fail to differentiate their markets and create nonspecific marketing for everyone, or they create approaches to segments based on their own product-centric view of the world.

Think about the websites you've visited. Have you noticed that sometimes you can glance at a site (or product page) and instantly know that it will not be helpful? I experience that feeling nearly every day. I might be shopping for something—say, a hotel for a family vacation in Tobago. So I go to Google and just search. Because I'm in the research phase of my decision, I'm looking for a site that will educate and inform me, not one that is chock-full of jargon and hype. I'm browsing and not ready to buy, so I'm not interested in a sales come-on. I'm expecting that the people who built the site have anticipated my need for helpful information. Yes, I am interested in booking a room at some point, but not until someone educates me about my options. What should I look for in Tobago? Should I be on the beach? Which beach? What's the trade-off between an all-inclusive versus à la carte experience? What's the price range? What are the advantages of a big resort compared with a small, intimate inn?

Usually I sample a few sites that are just terrible, filled with gobbledygook and corporate drivel. When that happens, I'm gone in a split second, clicking away, never to return. You know what I'm talking about, right? You make a decision immediately. It's a gut feeling, isn't it?

In contrast, a few sites have valuable and useful information. In fact, sometimes I feel that a site has been developed especially for me! It's as if someone read my mind and built a site based on my needs. The information I wanted was right there when I wanted to find it, telling me everything I needed to know.

It's not a coincidence when it feels like a company's marketing message and content was created especially for you. It means a marketer somewhere did his or her job well. It means that they took the time to understand their buyers' goals, needs, and objections. This isn't one of those egotistical companies that doesn't care about its customers. When the company takes the time to understand my questions and answer them through a video, a few blog posts, or a Q&A, I trust that company. And guess where I am inclined to buy? Yes, the place that was helpful, even if their price is higher than their competition's.

Adele Revella taught me about buyer personas nearly a decade ago, and it was one of the most important revelations I've had as a marketer. If you've read any of my recent bestselling books or seen one of my live presentations, you know I talk a lot about buyer personas. The concept of buyer personas is so essential to good marketing and sales that I've been bugging Adele to write this book for years. And I'm glad she did. Once you dig into the concept of buyer personas, you too will learn how to transform your marketing and your business.

You'll learn that buyer persona research ensures that you market using the voice of your buyer, not of your founder, CEO, product manager, or public relations (PR) agency staffer. This builds a bond of trust with your buyers that leads them into the buying process, making your salespeople's work easier and quicker.

Organizations that take the time to understand their buyer personas escape the trap of selling to the wrong people at the wrong time. You will see that by being helpful and informative rather than hyping, your marketing will come alive. Your buyer will be eager to do business with you and excited to share your ideas with others. The sale will be made more quickly, and your buyers may even be willing to pay a premium to work with you.

Gaining insight into your buyer personas will transform your business!

—David Meerman Scott
International bestselling author of *The New Rules of Marketing & PR* and *The New Rules of Sales and Service*
www.WebInkNow.com
twitter.com/dmscott

Acknowledgments

First, I want to thank the thousands of marketers who attended my product marketing workshops between 2001 and 2010. If you were among that audience, your plea for practical guidance about buyer personas was the inspiration for the training and research company that I founded in 2010 and ultimately, the reason that I wrote this book. I have faithfully attempted to answer your questions and trust that you will let me know if I have missed anything.

I am also deeply indebted to David Meerman Scott, whose best-selling books and frequent conference appearances are among the reasons that marketers around the world are clamoring for buyer personas. You were right, David; I needed to get these words out of my head and onto paper. I only wish it had been as easy as you described.

Many thanks to my clients, friends, and colleagues for sharing your stories about working with buyer personas. I had hoped to include everything you said and apologize to those whose tales are not included here. Sadly, there was space for only some of your hard-won wisdom.

This brings me to Lana Bradford. You were an incredible coach throughout this effort, and especially in those final weeks, as my ability to construct legible sentences was obscured by a rapidly approaching deadline. I could not have written this book without your skillful coaxing, extensive research, and clarifying edits.

Thank you to Shannon Vargo and Elizabeth Gildea at John Wiley & Sons for believing in this book and entrusting me with its writing. I am honored to be one of your authors.

I also want to acknowledge my fantastic team at Buyer Persona Institute, especially John Fox, Gordana Stok, Dave Barnhart, Frank Della Rosa, and Bonnie Wooding. It was through your commitment and hard work that the research kept flowing and the clients remained delighted in spite of my "book brain." You are amazing and I am privileged to work with you.

Finally, I want to thank my friends and family, whose faith in my ability to complete this work never flagged. In particular, I owe a debt of gratitude to Betsy Ruth Dayton for the gentle touch that kept my stress at a manageable level, and to our beloved dogs, Arie and Charlie, for insisting that it was time to stop writing and take a walk.

Most of all, I am grateful to my husband, Steve, for your partnership throughout this particular journey and all those that are yet to come. You are my rock.

Introduction
Listen First, Then Speak

"So what brings you in here to see me?"

That question is spoken countless times every day in doctors' offices, car repair shops, bank loan offices, law firms, and hundreds of other professional establishments. What usually follows that question is the customer's narrative describing their problem.

"My daughter is entering college next year, and I want to explore loan options for her education."

"It's probably nothing, doctor, but I've been wondering about a small change I've noticed recently . . ."

"The engine has been making the strangest sound when I drive downhill. It all started right after I loaned the car to my brother-in-law, who said he used it to move his large collection of Civil War cannon balls."

"I'm concerned that my cat has been pacing back and forth at night and making very loud howls."

Listening is an essential part of any first meeting. It's how professionals learn about their customers' concerns, goals, and expectations so that they can present a relevant solution.

Yet in many organizations this one-to-one communication between marketing professionals and their customers is infrequent—if it happens at all.

How often do you have an opportunity to listen to your customers describe their problems? Do you know how to ask the questions that will make this conversation valuable for you and your customer? And most important, do you know how to apply what you've heard to become a more effective marketer?

The art and science of asking probing questions and carefully listening to your customers' responses lie at the core of the buyer persona concept. It's the key to discovering their mind-set and the motivation that prompts them to purchase a solution like yours.

One marketing professional confessed to me after conducting her first buyer interview, "This is almost like cheating; like getting the exam paper weeks before the final. Instead of trying to guess what matters, I now know not only what the customer wants—I realize how she goes about it."

This is the power of the buyer persona. Built around a story about your customers' buying decision, the buyer persona reveals insight into your buyer's expectations and concerns as they decide whether to do business with you, choose your competitor, or simply opt to do nothing at all.

This book will show you how you can listen to your buyers' stories to gain insight into the factors that trigger their search, how they define success, and what affects their final decision that a particular approach is the best one for them. We'll show you how the buyer's personal narrative reveals language and phrases that will resonate with other buyers with similar concerns, and how to define and focus on the activities that compel buyers to take action. You will see how giving buyers the clearly articulated information they seek, in the language they understand, when and where they need it, is the essence of effective marketing.

Why Is Everyone Talking about Buyer Personas?

In the simplest terms, buyer personas are examples or archetypes of real buyers that allow marketers to craft strategies to promote products and services to the people who might buy them. During the past decade the term has almost become a marketing mantra.

But as this book will show, the growing interest in buyer personas has resulted in confusion about how they are created, how they are used, and their ultimate effectiveness.

It's the intention of this book to provide some much needed clarity.

The marketer's need to understand the market is hardly new. But the depth of insight required is increasing exponentially as technological advances demand that organizations rethink how they sell everything from music and books to bulldozers and information technology. Michael Gottlieb, a senior director of marketing and business strategy at one of the world's leading software firms, described it this way: "*What* we are selling is changing; *who* we are selling to is changing (some are people we've never sold to before); and *how* these customers want to be engaged, marketed, and sold to is changing, too."

Buyer personas have a lot to do with attaining that kind of alignment, but not in the way that marketers often use them, which is basically to build a profile of the people who are their intended customers. Rather, the contention of this book is that when buyer personas evolve from authentic stories related by actual buyers—*in the form of one-on-one interviews*—the methodology and presentation allows you to capture the buyer's expectations and the factors that influence them. Then, and only then, can you truly stand in your buyer's shoes and consider the buying decision from the buyer's point of view. This goes way beyond buyer profiling—but most marketers don't realize that.

As a veteran sales and marketing executive, trainer, and researcher, I've worked with thousands of marketers in hundreds of companies. Not long ago, I met with executives from a large corporation who had spent hundreds of thousands of dollars for research on "buyer personas" that was essentially worthless. The company had purchased profiles about the people who buy from it, but these failed to capture the crucially important stories revealing how buyers make this type of decision. I've also seen companies purchase oversegmented research that defined dozens of buyer personas, a number that would be feasibly impossible for them to market to with any effectiveness.

In both of these cases, the company had lost its way by focusing on the goal to build buyer personas without a clear plan to ensure that they contain useful findings.

Naturally, it's far easier to make educated guesses and assumptions about what buyers may be thinking based on extrapolations of your own knowledge or intuition. That's certainly how large aspects of the marketing community have functioned for decades. But the climate of social and technological change favors companies that embrace a culture of buyer understanding that allows them to adapt to customer needs. Just consider the major technology players that have receded or disappeared: AOL, Digital, Polaroid, Wang, AltaVista, Netscape, Fairchild Semiconductor, Palm, Sun Microsystems. The list could run for pages. Each of these companies was outrun by competitors who possessed greater clarity about their buyers' expectations.

Will This Approach Work for You?

This book is for marketing executives who wish to avoid that kind of dire scenario, whether they work in the business-to-business (B2B) or the business-to-consumer (B2C) arena. It is specifically aimed at marketers of "medium- and high-consideration" products, services, and solutions—buying decisions that require a considerable investment of your buyers' thought and time. Examples of high-consideration decisions range from selecting the right vendor of capital equipment or picking which college to attend to carefully choosing a new car or the most appropriate location for office space. This decision-making process differs markedly from impulse purchases made in a grocery store or at the checkout register.

When you consider that we want to interview buyers to capture their story, it is easy to understand why a detailed narrative about a choice between exotic vacation destinations would be immensely useful. In contrast, little insight would be gained as a result of asking a buyer to explain why she decided to purchase a particular pack of gum.

Although the Internet has given us instant access to immense knowledge, even the most sophisticated applications of Big Data won't reveal what you can learn by listening to your buyers' stories. Just as there is nothing to acquaint you with a foreign culture as intimately as staying with a native family in their home, the best way to gain deep insight into the mind-set of your buyers is to spend quality time with them.

The buyer persona methodology outlined in this book will help companies avoid the consequences that inevitably engulf organizations that fail to listen intensely to their buyers. In the pages to come I will explain how you can use buyer personas to craft successful marketing strategies based on insight that would otherwise be nearly impossible to acquire. I will show how this can be done without exorbitant investments in money, time, or labor. It just requires adhering to a well-defined process, mastering a few skills, and honing your analytical thinking. This is a craft and a set of skills that can be learned, and this book will serve as your primer for how you or your organization can achieve this.

We've organized this book into three parts. In the first three chapters, you'll learn what a buyer persona is and what it is not. You'll find out why so many buyer personas are not as useful as they should be and what you need to do to ensure the success of your buyer persona initiative.

In Part II, we'll help you decide whether you want to build your own buyer personas or use a third party to do this work for you. You'll learn about every aspect of the methodology that you or your contractor needs to employ to interview buyers about their decisions, collect and analyze your findings, and use these to build insightful buyer personas.

Finally, in Part III, we'll share step-by-step guidance about how to use buyer personas to define your marketing strategies. You'll learn how to rely on buyer persona insights to develop your messaging and marketing activities and align with your sales organization, and in the final chapter, we'll recommend a place to begin and explain our vision for the future role of buyer personas.

We are excited that you share our interest in buyer personas and hope that this book will help you join the growing ranks of buyer expert marketers.

PART I

Understanding the Art and Science of Buyer Personas

1 | Understand Buying Decisions and the People Who Make Them

The launch of Apple's iPhone in January 2007 is now widely recognized as a pivotal moment in the history of digital technology and consumer culture. When it went on sale later that year, customers in the United States and parts of Europe greeted the iPhone with near rapture.

A few months later, during the summer of 2008, Apple introduced the iPhone 3G in a total of 22 countries. But what happened to the iPhone in technology-obsessed Japan is a classic lesson in the importance of deeply understanding the expectations of buyers.

Incredibly, Apple hadn't considered that buyers in the Japanese market might have different needs from U.S. and European buyers. And the results were compelling.

Although demand for the iPhone exceeded supply in many other parts of the world, in Japan the iPhone 3G was gathering dust on store shelves by the close of 2008. Press reports the following spring indicated that Japanese sales of the iPhone were only 200,000 units, primarily to existing users of Apple computers and laptops. This was a country where an estimated 50 million cell phones had been sold the previous year.

With a minimum of research, Apple could have discovered that by 2008 the Japanese were accustomed to using their personal phones to shoot videos and to watch digital TV programs. Yet the iPhone 3G didn't even include a video camera. What's more, Apple could have anticipated the difficulty competing in a market where many phones routinely included chips for debit card transactions and train passes. After all, Japan is a place where trains are a part of daily life, and credit cards are rarely accepted. Debit transactions are the primary currency.

To compound the situation, the iPhone was also more expensive than its competitors in Japan. Perhaps Apple thought that its online software store would be valuable enough to justify the higher price. If only the company had known that its target buyers were reluctant to shop online in 2008.

This was nearly the end of the story for the iPhone in Japan. "A lot of times, people don't know what they want until you show it to them," Steve Jobs boldly proclaimed to *Businessweek* in an interview a decade earlier. Having seen the iPhone 3G, the Japanese market had shown Apple's brilliant visionary CEO what they didn't want, as well as the dangers of relying exclusively on intuition and past success as a marketing strategy.

Luckily, Apple learned its lesson. Four years later *Forbes* reported that the iPhone 5s had captured 34 percent of the Japanese smartphone market, in a country now widely considered as the world's most sophisticated, advanced, and competitive marketplace for smartphones.

The dramatic difference this time: Apple was keenly aware of what its Japanese buyers were expecting.

Apple is fortunate to be that rare brand with the resources to recover from such a stumble. Nonetheless, it would have been far less costly in terms of time, expense, labor, and brand reputation for Apple to have interviewed Japanese buyers about their smartphone expectations before this launch.

Why the "Know Your Customer" Rule Has Been Redefined

The story of Apple's iPhone launch in Japan reminds us that even the most admired companies cannot avoid one of the most basic rules of business: Know your customer.

Now that customers are choosing how and when they will engage with your sales and marketing efforts, this timeless truth is gaining new urgency, forcing companies to reconsider their approach to discovering and applying customer insight.

In 2012, the Corporate Executive Board's (CEB) Marketing Leadership Council released a widely cited study that concisely defined the problem, revealing that on average, business-to-business (B2B) customers are nearly 60 percent of the way through the purchase decision before engaging a sales representative. There is compelling evidence that customers of business-to-consumer (B2C) companies are equally likely to rely on peers and digital connections to guide their decisions about what to buy and which supplier they should trust.

We know that the 60 percent statistic cited in the CEB study is not universally applicable, but the trend is unmistakable—customers who have the resources and networks to make buying decisions without your input are happy to do so.

> Armed with instant access to countless peer-reviewed options, customers are holding your sales and marketing teams to a new standard: Tell me what I want to know and help me find the right option at every stage of my buying decision, or I'll go somewhere else.

This change in customer decision making is a game changer for companies that have always relied on their salespeople to listen to each buyer's needs and create a winning argument, one customer at a time, while marketers stayed inside the building, churning out marketing materials and running campaigns that were based on a good deal of supposition about what their customers wanted to hear. If we start with the principle that effective communication requires good listening, it's easy to see that marketers have been working with a severe and illogical handicap.

Although the details about buyer personas are unclear to many, their goal is simple. Marketers must understand how markets full of buyers navigate the buying decision they want to influence so that they can become a useful, trusted resource throughout that decision. Marketers need to become good listeners if they want to be effective communicators.

A Clothes Dryer's Extra Setting Made All the Difference

Beko, a Turkish manufacturer of major household consumer appliances, took a very different tack than the Apple team that launched the iPhone 4 in Japan. They prepared for a launch into the lucrative and unfamiliar Chinese market by listening to buyers of electric clothes dryers.

According to David Meerman Scott, who visited with Beko executives in Istanbul in 2014, Beko staffers routinely conduct in-depth interviews with potential customers before introducing an appliance in any international market. In the course of their conversations with buyers in China, Beko marketers learned that many people hold fast to a cultural tradition that uses direct sunlight to dry clothes. Some Chinese believe there is a spiritual component when garments are exposed to the sun. So rather than throw in the towel (so to speak), Beko dryers were built with a setting that stops the drying cycle when it is only half done. Now Beko consumers can partially dry their wet laundry and then hang the slightly damp clothing in the sunlight.

Scott reports that the new Beko dryers are just one of their appliances that are selling very well in the Chinese market. Chinese buyer interviews led Beko to design a refrigerator that is very different from those routinely sold in Western countries. As almost everyone knows, rice is part of the daily Chinese diet. Without the research, however, Beko might not have known that their buyers wanted a refrigerator that could store rice at low humidity and a temperature of 10 degrees Celsius, a setting that's too warm for conventional refrigerated food. So Beko's Chinese model has three doors instead of the familiar two, each with separate temperature and humidity controls. Scott reported that "at the 2013 IFA Fair, the world's leading trade show for consumer electronics and home appliances, this Beko refrigerator won a coveted innovation award."

Luckily, most marketers don't have to confront cultural factors as unusual as those that affected the introduction of Apple and Beko's products in Asia. But the essential concern—the importance of focusing on the concerns and expectations of your buyers—remains a crucial issue for all marketers, even those whose buyers live right next door. And admittedly, for many marketers their buyers' mind-sets can be as mysterious as the customs of citizens living in a foreign country.

It wasn't necessary for Apple and Beko to engage the methodology behind building buyer personas to avoid stumbling in their new markets. Some basic old-fashioned consumer market research was involved. But the fact that Beko undertook a concerted effort to interview their prospective Chinese customers demonstrates the wisdom of a disciplined approach to gathering insights into buyer expectations.

Will You Understand Your Buyers' Decisions?

Most buying decisions are not as easily understood as those in the Apple iPhone and Beko examples. Many buying decisions are far more complex, involving many variables and multiple influencers or decision makers. Geographic distinctions may or may not alter the buyer's approach to the decision. And product design modifications are an uncommon result of building buyer personas.

However, the most crucial aspect of buyer personas applies to each of these stories: The companies involved needed to listen to their buyers tell a story about a considered decision.

We will explore other circumstances and approaches in Chapter 3, but the most effective way to build buyer personas is to interview buyers who have previously weighed their options, considered or rejected solutions, and made a decision similar to the one you want to influence. Unfortunately, many marketers don't realize that hearing and relating their customer's story is the foundation of understanding them as a buyer. So it's essential to clearly define what a buyer persona is—and what it is not.

In some marketing courses and websites, buyer personas are defined as something similar to Figure 1.1.

Here we see Jim, a fictional archetype who is meant to represent a typical operations manager. The graphic outline gives us information about Jim's education, age, to whom he reports, his skills, the

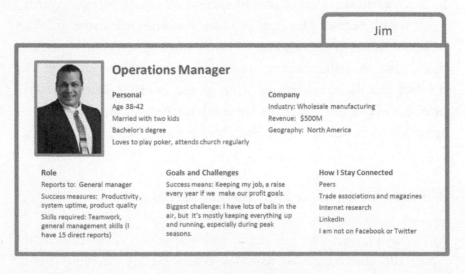

Figure 1.1   Example Buyer Profile

incentives and rewards from his job (keeping his job and an occasional raise), and how he spends his free time (family, church, a weekly poker game with his friends); plus how he stays current on the latest trends in his industry, broken down into four categories. This is a Buyer Profile that is heavy on data that could be readily gleaned from online sources.

What does this tell us about how Jim makes a buying decision? We see he reads industry publications, belongs to industry trade groups, and uses the Internet when searching for solutions. Alas, the same could be said for about 99 percent of other business professionals working at a comparable managerial level.

Let's say Jim is looking for a new logistics management supplier. From this template, what do we know about what's motivating Jim to find a new supplier? What does he expect to be different once he makes this switch? What is very important to Jim about the appearance of the packaging and enclosures in the shipments sent to retailers? What does Jim dislike about a lot of the providers he has used in the past?

Marketers hoping to interest Jim in their logistics services using his Buyer Profile template won't find much useful intelligence here. Instead they would need to use this profile to imagine (guess?) how Jim would respond to their messaging when sitting at his desk.

It's difficult to imagine how this approach to buyer personas will help marketers of logistics solutions know what they need to do to help Jim see their solution as a perfect fit for his needs. Furthermore, it is unlikely that this company's marketers will use this tool to persuade their internal stakeholders that a different approach to their messaging and marketing activities will set their merchandise or services apart from their competition.

Buyer Profiles will not transform this marketer's ability to think like Jim. But suppose you knew what Jim is looking for when he is considering signing a contract with a new provider, why he has been dissatisfied with other providers in the past, and a score of other specific details about how Jim makes his decision. And suppose that these actionable details are things that neither you, nor your own salespeople, nor the competition has ever heard before.

Relying on Buyer Demographics and Psychographics

Too often, Buyer Profiles are nothing more than an attractive way to display obvious or demographic data. Defining markets based on demographics—data such as a person's age, income, marital status, and education—is the legacy of 60 years of selling to the mass market.

When large-circulation magazines and network television were marketing to the public *en masse*, demographics helped them create market segments that could be targeted by their advertisers and program managers. Many companies, especially those that market retail consumer products, still rely on demographics to define their markets.

Yet such distinctions can be irrelevant, if not misleading, when applied in many instances of persuasive marketing. Since marketers have been using demographics for generations to define and segment their buyers—often with very productive results—it requires some attention to realize they are not the best way to build buyer personas.

Some marketers will focus on psychographics, another long-standing approach to segmenting markets based on factors such as personality, values, lifestyles, and opinions. This approach might capture the fact that Jim goes to church regularly, is skilled at managing people, and is challenged by keeping multiple balls in the air. But this information has little bearing on how he will evaluate and choose a logistics management supplier. Combined with a few demographics, you might know the kind of neighborhood he lives in and that he likes to spend time with his family, but you'll still have to guess about what triggers his interest to evaluate your solution, the barriers that prevent him from finalizing the purchase, and which of your advantages will impress him.

How Marketers Benefit from Buyer Profiles

The Buyer Profile has gained a lot of traction because it is a useful tool to help you think about your target buyers as real people, with actual families, typical bosses, and human concerns. For the same reason that we find it far easier to communicate via social media when we have a photograph of a person we have never met in person, the Buyer Profile creates a sense of the human connection with people whom we have never met face-to-face. If you've ever built a relationship with someone through social media, you may have noticed that your first in-person encounter feels a lot like running into an old friend. The photograph and details of this person's job or personal life have likely shaped your interactions and created a sense of intimacy despite the fact that you live and work in very different circumstances.

Marketers who may never meet the chief financial officer at a large bank can rely on the Buyer Profile to understand why trying to reach him through an email marketing campaign is so difficult.

Marketers who get the most benefit from Buyer Profiles are those who find it easy to imagine themselves making the decision they want to influence. Consider the story of Jessica.

Some years ago an advertising agency constructed a detailed Buyer Profile to describe the person who was the typical buyer of their client's car. The profile detailed the tastes, lifestyle, attitudes, and concerns of a buyer they named "Jessica." This team wasn't satisfied with a slide deck or poster describing Jessica; they actually created a "Jessica room" containing the Ikea furniture that she would use to decorate her apartment, a glass coffee table displaying the magazines she would read, and a goldfish tank, knickknacks, and small television on the bookshelf.

I have never heard of anyone else who has allocated actual office space to their buyer persona, but it's easy to see that being seated in this room would help the agency's marketers remember that a real woman like Jessica was the target of their marketing strategies. In this environment, a suggestion to emphasize the spaciousness of the car's cargo area for large dogs or landscape materials would be easily discarded, as the marketers were clearly aware that Jessica was rarely home (goldfish require little maintenance) and she certainly has no time or space for a garden.

Buying Insights Complete Your Persona

For many marketers, the demographic profile is the beginning and end of their buyer persona's story. But marketers gain far more value from buyer personas when they include their buyer's story about the decision they want to influence.

What if the agency marketers for Jessica's car had repurposed the budget and time they'd allocated to her apartment and used it to interview real customers about their car-buying decisions? By listening to in-depth stories related by buyers like Jessica, the agency would have known what triggered Jessica's decision to skip her Saturday aerobics class to look for a new car. Rather than guessing (and second-guessing) which aspects of their cars she'd evaluate, the agency could have asked real buyers how they justified the extra cost of optional packages. Most critically, they would have clearly understood the barriers that prevented her from including their client's dealerships in her Saturday visits.

The agency marketers could have benefited from building buyer personas that included two parts: a Buyer Profile that describes Jessica, and Buying Insights, describing the when, how, and why aspects of Jessica's decision to buy a car.

Unlike the simple categories that typify a Buyer Profile, your buyer's story is a lengthy narrative related through the personal buying experiences of people like those you want to influence. Although the concept is simple, there are many things you will want to know about whom to interview, how to engage them in telling their story, and how to build a cohesive, actionable Buyer Persona based on your findings.

In Part II of this book you'll learn how to find people to interview, conduct a probing interview, and mine those interviews to communicate the Buying Insights that you and your company need to make effective marketing decisions. You will need to read several chapters to learn how to achieve this result, but it is easy to explain what you'll learn through Buying Insights, and to see why this will be the most actionable part of your buyer persona.

Buying Insights reveal:

- Which buyers are receptive, and which will ignore you no matter what you say
- Which aspects of your solution are relevant to them, and which are irrelevant
- What attitudes prevent your buyers from considering your solutions
- What resources your buyers trust as they evaluate their options
- Which buyers are involved in the decision and how much influence they wield

A Buyer Profile alone allows you to focus on who your buyer is through demographic data assigned to a fictional name and portrait. When you combine the Buyer Profile with Buying Insights, you will have clear guidance for the decisions you need to make to win their business. Companies that are fully invested in this approach can mention Jim in a meeting and evoke the full story about what the company needs to do to persuade him.

High-Consideration Decisions Reveal the Best Insights

Some buyer stories reveal more insight than others, and you may be surprised to learn that this question has nothing to do with whether you are a B2B or B2C marketer.

When people make a high-consideration buying decision—think about a consumer purchasing a home or an executive investing in capital equipment—they invest an enormous amount of time and energy evaluating their options. Some decisions take only a period of days; others take weeks; and some take months or even years. Whether it's a large corporation's information executive evaluating a new technology architecture or parents considering a college for their son or daughter, these decisions require a substantial financial investment, and the outcome of the decision will profoundly affect the lives of others well into the future. The buyers are engaged in a thorough analysis of the various options before they arrive at a conclusion. Typically they will also need to be able to defend or discuss that decision with others who will have to live with the consequences, for better or worse.

Contrast this kind of decision with the improbability of discerning how that same person might approach a low-consideration choice— such as selecting one brand of soap from a shelf containing an array of options—and you can see why Buying Insights are more readily available to marketers of medium- to high-consideration solutions.

As we will discuss briefly in Chapter 3, low-consideration buying decisions are best understood through complex algorithms that examine the buyer's online behavior, or through costly choice modeling and ethnographic studies that attempt to examine mind-sets that people cannot explain, even to themselves.

Marketers of high-consideration solutions are fortunate that a technique as simple as the one in this book reveals even greater insight. If you are in this category, your buyer's conscientious investment in this decision makes it possible for you to deeply understand the logical and emotional aspects of a decision you have never personally encountered.

A person's thoughts about an impulsive or low-consideration buying decision usually reside in the realm of the unconscious. Conversely, high-consideration buying decisions involve, by definition, considerable conscious thought that can be expressed, evaluated, and analyzed.

You can see that grocery store consumers making low-consideration decisions would be unable to explain precisely how and why they chose one product off the shelf rather than another. If you asked this buyer to tell a story about that decision, you would be unlikely to gain real insight. But that same individual can tell you fascinating and revealing stories about how they chose an architect for their new home, or how they planned an elaborate wedding.

All marketers gain value from listening to their buyers. But we can see that as individuals invest more time and effort thinking about a challenge or solution, they simultaneously become more acutely aware of the journey they have undertaken and the steps they followed to reach their conclusion. Active contemplation and reflection that took place over an extended period of time is far, far easier to recount than trying to recapture the dynamics behind decisions made quickly and then seldom revisited.

Buying Insights from a Quick Trip to London

Probing interviews with buyers who engaged in medium- or high-consideration decisions invariably reveal insight that no one in your company has heard. Time and again, we have seen how these interviews uncover previously unknown information that makes a decisive difference—factors that direct the company to achieve unexpected success or, as this story examines, prevent a costly misstep that would have embarrassed everyone. Although you may not be happy about what you learn through your buyer interviews, in some situations even bad news can make you a hero.

A few years ago a technology firm asked me to help them prepare for the launch of an entirely new solution that was nearly complete. With partial funding by a major client, this tech company had developed a Web portal that would streamline the day-to-day processing of an arcane and litigious area of maritime law. One of the oldest forms of international jurisprudence, admiralty law covers marine commerce, navigation, salvaging, shipping, and the transportation of passengers and goods. A single dispute generally involves multiple parties—the owner of cargo, the shipping company, the port, the buyer, those damaged in an accident, and many more—so the paperwork can be formidable.

My assignment was to identify which of the decision makers at these organizations were most receptive to this solution and, most critically, how the costs would be distributed among them. We needed to understand the triggers that would motivate them to use the portal, which of many benefits were most relevant, and how we could efficiently reach these very different buyers with sales and marketing activities. Our client expected that insights into their buyers' concerns and expectations would result in rapid adoption of their new portal.

I was fortunate that the industry would soon be gathering in London for its annual conference about this specific niche of admiralty law, and convinced the client that my attendance would produce quick results. I wasn't wrong. Between sessions, I found the participants were happy to talk about the processes they were currently using and that it was easy to get their reaction to the concept of my client's portal. In 22 interviews I found unanimity. But what I discovered was not what the software developer was hoping to learn.

Far from embracing a solution that would coordinate and streamline the massive paperwork that consumed their professional lives, the buyers were adamantly opposed to it. "There is no way I would use anything like a Web portal," they told me in one interview after another.

I was astonished. It was 2009 and yet here was a large group of global businesspeople whose mind-set was entrenched in laws and business practices that hadn't changed in more than a century. A relatively simple solution that would have minimized paperwork, eased communications, and prevented litigation ran into the hard reality of a complex network of business practices and people who were fundamentally resistant to technology and change.

It was a truly frustrating reality. And it was certainly no fun delivering the message to my client that, for now at least, these buyers were not interested in using my client's portal, even if it were free. I was gratified that they welcomed my findings, noting the embarrassment and financial losses they would have incurred with a solution that the industry saw as inappropriate or irrelevant.

Rather bluntly, my client told me that the disappointing situation revealed during the course of my buyer persona interviews had actually saved the company millions of dollars. It's worth remembering that many good products have been developed at a time before the market is ready for them. The first tablet computer and first e-book readers went on sale years before the market was prepared to embrace them and before the technology was able to deliver the experience that buyers wanted. Alas, the companies who were first to market are no longer in business.

Everyone would agree that knowing your buyers' mind-set in detail—even when the reality can be as disappointing as what I discovered at the London conference—is preferable to sitting around a table and playing the old marketing guessing game. But to create effective buyer personas with actionable Buying Insights requires learning a unique methodology, engaging with your buyers, listening to their stories, and mastering some interviewing and analytical skills.

In the pages ahead we'll discuss these in detail and tell you how you too can be a buyer persona expert.

2 | Focus on the Insights That Guide Marketing Decisions

"Eureka!"

For more than two millennia, that single word has been associated with the most celebrated "aha!" moment in history. It was the shout spoken by the ancient Greek mathematician Archimedes as he jumped from his bathtub and excitedly ran naked through the streets of Syracuse. Archimedes had just realized that he could calculate the volume of an irregular object by measuring how much water it displaced.

Whether the citizens of Syracuse found this public display anything out of the ordinary is lost to history, but the story makes it clear that a moment of insight is worth celebrating.

By comparison, knowledge is merely interesting. You read a book or attend a class and often learn something that you will soon forget. And then suddenly, an encounter as ordinary as Archimedes's daily bath produces a new insight, a fantastic moment when all of the pieces of a once inscrutable puzzle fall into place. If you have experienced these flashes of insight, we don't need to explain their power to motivate and inspire.

Perhaps you are attending a conference at which a keynote speaker clarifies a problem you have contemplated at length. You suddenly see how you could take a different approach and attain a goal that was critical to your company. Thrilled with your discovery, you turn to the colleague seated next to you, fully expecting his smile to match your own. Instead, he is preoccupied with his phone. When you have a chance to share what you heard, he is unimpressed. Amazing. When you return to your company the reactions are similar. Your resolve weakens, and you may even conclude that you should abandon your plan.

It is easy to imagine that the townspeople in ancient Greece had a similar reaction to Archimedes's mathematical breakthrough. Without the unique background and focus on the problem that had plagued Archimedes, it would be difficult for the citizens of Syracuse to understand the implications and join in his celebration. Those who related the story to their friends undoubtedly failed to explain the insight or its implications.

These stories give us a glimpse of the importance of insights and how they are distinct from ordinary knowledge. More critically, they caution us to carefully consider how we use insights to influence the people around us. We wonder how many times the benefits of a remarkable discovery were delayed or entirely lost due to a failure to communicate it effectively.

In 1983, a software developer broke ranks with traditional design methodologies to rely on customer insight as the foundation for a new product. When success required him to communicate those insights to teams, he had an inspiration that is the foundation of effective product design and marketing.

Listening to Kathy

When Alan Cooper sat down to design a new project management software program, he was wrestling with a troubling problem. He instinctively knew that software should be designed to meet users' needs, but at that time, programmers were very technically oriented people who were building products that users found intimidating. Searching for guidance on a user-friendly design, he decided to interview an assortment of colleagues who seemed to be the software's likely end users.

What he learned from these user interviews resulted in the creation of an imaginary user—Kathy—a composite named after one of the people he interviewed. By thinking about Kathy, Cooper could speculatively project the concerns and expectations of his new software's users, and mentally imagine their reactions to the various ways that he might design the solution he was developing.

Cooper fell into an unusual daily work schedule that should inspire all of us who spend our days at our desks. Breaking out of his typical routine, Cooper would ponder the details of his new program during a lunchtime break that often involved an extended walk along the Old Del Monte golf course in Monterey.

In a recollection published a quarter of a century later, Cooper wrote:

> As I walked, I would engage myself in a dialogue, play-acting a project manager, loosely based on Kathy, requesting functions and behavior from my program. I often found myself deep in those dialogues, speaking aloud, and gesturing with my arms. Some of the golfers were taken aback by my unexpected presence and unusual behavior, but that didn't bother me because I found that this play-acting technique was remarkably effective for cutting through complex design questions of functionality and interaction, allowing me to clearly see what was necessary and unnecessary and, more importantly, to differentiate between what was used frequently and what was needed only infrequently.

The program that Cooper designed was both a critical and commercial triumph. Bolstered by this success, he employed it again while writing the software that would be the core of Visual Basic, the foundation for the graphical user interface behind Microsoft Windows 3.0. It was this reiteration of user-friendly drag-and-drop technology—first pioneered in the Macintosh—that swiftly became ubiquitous in offices around the world.

Frustrated, a Newly Minted Consultant Invents Personas

With this enormous success to his credit, Cooper abandoned his development career to become a consultant to companies that employed large teams of developers. To his dismay, he quickly learned that his ability to focus on the user's experience didn't occur naturally to others. Out of frustration with one of his clients, he conducted open-ended customer interviews and quickly identified that the developers needed to address the needs of three different types of users. Here is the result in Cooper's own words:

> At the next group meeting, I presented my designs from the points of view of Chuck, Cynthia, and Rob instead of from my own. The results were dramatic. While there was still resistance to this unfamiliar method, the programmers could clearly see the sense in my designs because they could identify with these hypothetical archetypes. From then on, I always presented design work using one of the personas, and eventually even the Sagent [Technologies] engineers began to talk about "what Cynthia would do" or "whether Chuck could understand" some dialog box.

In 1998 Cooper published the influential book *The Inmates Are Running the Asylum*, in which he offered a series of provocative and entertaining personal reflections to explain why talented people repeatedly design bad software. It was in its pages that Cooper introduced what became the first popularization of his method: "Personas are not real people, but they represent them throughout the design process. They are hypothetical archetypes of actual users. Although they are imaginary, they are defined with significant rigor and precision. Actually, we don't so much 'make up' our personas as discover them as a byproduct of the investigation process. We do, however, make up their names and personal details."

Cooper later proposed that his usage of personas was in essence counterlogical. He knew that it would be more logical to ask all of the members of the user community to submit their desired features, and then deliver a product that contained all of them. He also understood that this would result in a "pathetic" product. Thus his persona-based design solution arose outside of the world of academia. He realized that a tool that was practical for daily work was far more useful and rational than anything that he could produce through academic research.

He noted his ideas weren't an entirely original concept: "*Product marketing professionals have also been using persona-like entities for many years to define demographic segments. But personas are unique and uniquely effective.*"

Nearly two decades after *Inmates* was published, user personas and Cooper's design principles are a critical part of educational curriculum for product designers. By interviewing people similar to those who would use his new products, Cooper had access to insights that dramatically altered the quality of the product designs that he controlled. But his ability to persuade teams to take advice from their users was accomplished by aggregating those insights into a persona. For the first time, programmers located in every corner of the world were united by a cohesive understanding of the user's mind-set about the product they were developing.

It seems only fair that marketers should have this same advantage.

Buyers Have Distinct Expectations

It is in the pages of Cooper's *Inmates* that we see the first usage of the term "buyer persona." He wasn't predicting the future of buyer personas as we know them today, but making the distinction that buyers have different needs, expectations, and goals than users. His mention of buyer personas was a caution to software designers to separate customers into two categories—the "before purchase" buyer persona and the "after purchase" user persona. Although the primary goal for both types of personas is identical—to discover the customer insights that will help teams make good decisions—it is clear that development teams need very different insights than marketing teams.

Unfortunately, as buyer personas have evolved to include some of the excellent principles that Cooper originated to help designers, this evolution has also transferred ideas that are counterproductive for marketers. These practices have resulted in bloated personas that miss the key insights marketers need.

For example, one popular but misguided idea that has transferred from user to buyer personas is that they should describe a "day in the life" of the buyer. You can see why an engineer who is designing a solution that is used daily could benefit from insights about the user's day. These insights would certainly affect the product design and could even reveal the need for an entirely new innovation for that user.

But if you are marketing a high-consideration solution such as a vacation destination, you can just as easily see that your buyer persona's typical day is of little value. The same is true for the senior executive whom you hope to persuade to invest in your costly capital equipment. By definition, a high-consideration decision occurs infrequently and spans many days, weeks, months, or even years. A typical day would certainly not include any activity relevant to a decision like the one you want to influence.

On the other hand, this distinction means that it would be incredibly useful to know what happens on the one day that, unlike all others, your travel company's buyer persona decides to take a break from daily life and plan a big trip. Or imagine the value of knowing what changes occur on the day the plant manager's company decides to invest the time and budget to replace your category of production line equipment.

The 5 Rings of Buying Insight

When you know what triggers your buyer's decision to prioritize an investment in a solution like the one your organization offers, you have discovered the first of five Buying Insights that will help you align your marketing strategies with your buyer's expectations. With this and four additional insights, you will know what happens and who is involved as your buyers navigate from the status quo to purchase a solution like yours.

Insight 1—Priority Initiative

The Priority Initiative insight explains the most compelling reason that buyers decide to invest in a solution similar to the one your organization offers, and why others are content with the status quo. Because this insight describes in detail the personal or organizational circumstances that cause buyers to allocate their time, budget, or political capital to purchase a solution like yours, you know when buyers are receptive to hearing from you and which personas are triggering the decision to make this investment.

Marketers use this insight to define, defend, and execute strategies that resonate with buyers at the earliest stages in their decision.

Insight 2—Success Factors

The Success Factors insight describes the operational or personal results that your buyer persona expects from purchasing a solution like yours. Success Factors resemble benefits, but this insight eliminates the need to guess at or reverse-engineer your messaging based on your solution's capabilities. For example, where you might be emphasizing your solution's power to cut costs, this insight might tell you that your buyer is more concerned about reducing business risks. Or you might learn that your consumer buyer is motivated by a desire to control something specific about his or her environment.

Through this insight, you would know exactly which risks are most worrisome and how your buyers describe the rewards of achieving control.

Insight 3—Perceived Barriers

We often refer to Perceived Barriers as the "bad news" insight because it tells you what prevents buyers from considering your solution—as well as why some believe that your competitors have a better approach. The barrier may reflect internal resistance from another decision maker or an unfortunate prior experience with similar solutions. It could be a negative perception of your product or company, accurate or not.

When you know where the barriers are and who's behind them, you know what you need to do to reassure your buyer that your company or solution will help achieve their Priority Initiative and Success Factors.

Insight 4—Buyer's Journey

This insight reveals the behind-the-scenes story about the work your buyers do to evaluate options, eliminate contenders, and settle on their final choice. Through this insight, you will know which of several influencers is involved at each phase of the decision, what they did to arrive at their conclusions, and how much influence each of them has over the decision.

You will use the Buyer's Journey insight to align your sales and marketing activities to target the most influential buyers at each phase of the decision, through resources that help them see your approach as a perfect fit for their needs.

Insight 5—Decision Criteria

Through Decision Criteria, you will learn about the specific attributes of your product, service, or solution that buyers evaluate as they compare alternative approaches. Decision Criteria insights frequently surprise marketers by revealing that buyers are not satisfied with benefits-oriented marketing materials, and that companies that communicate facts are more likely to gain their buyers' trust. You may even learn that your newest or most distinctive capabilities have the least impact on their decision.

Give Your Buyer a Seat at the Table

The 5 Rings of Buying Insight serve as guardrails for your marketing team, keeping everyone in your company on track to make profitable decisions about how to reach and persuade the buyers who have a need for solutions like the one your organization is offering. When these insights are expressed through verbatim quotes from actual buyers, they tell a compelling story about what your buyers want to hear and where they are seeking information as they weigh their options. Now marketing has the credibility to lead teams to make decisions that align with their buyers' needs, goals, and concerns.

Part III of this book is dedicated to a detailed exploration of the various ways buyer personas can guide effective, defensible marketing decisions. In advance, however, here is a brief preview that explains how Buying Insights can help address many of the top challenges that marketers are facing today.

Creating Effective Messaging

Marketers of high-consideration solutions have always found the creation of engaging messages and meaningful copy a struggle. The benefits of a complex solution cannot be easily distilled into few words or sentences. It's nearly impossible to construct meaningful statements that can quickly and succinctly explain a long list of advantages and the values a solution delivers. If that wasn't enough, this messaging also needs to be understood by anyone. As a result, marketers fall into the habit of using words such as "market-leading," "flexible," "scalable," and "easy-to-use."

When marketers have insight into their buyers' expectations, they know which buyers their message needs to persuade and which of the many attributes of their solution are the most important to each buyer's decision. Armed with verbatim quotes describing how buyers weigh their options and make a choice, marketers can readily find the sweet spot between their buyer's needs and their solution's capabilities.

Generating High-Quality Leads

Among a marketer's top priorities is the need to improve the quality of leads while simultaneously sustaining a high volume. However, we're seeing even greater urgency around this objective now that buyers are more than 60 percent through a buying decision by the time they contact the supplier directly. It is no longer good enough to create awareness; marketers must convince buyers that their solution should remain among the short list of finalists whose salespeople will be invited to meet with the prospect.

Marketers who have insight into their buyers' priorities, expectations, and preferred resources know where their buyers are looking for guidance, the questions they're asking, and most critically, which answers they want to hear. This combination of insights informs decisions about the kind of information buyers want to consume and how to place it where buyers are looking.

Shortening the Sales Cycle; Speed to Revenue

This challenge is showing up on the list of high-priority marketing objectives as a result of management's goal to align its sales and marketing organizations. As soon as marketing is accountable for revenue results, the pressure is on for marketing to do more than generate leads and build the usual sales tools. There is an expectation that marketing should partner with sales to help close deals faster.

Marketers who listen to buyers describe their buying decision have a chance to peer inside the inner workings of their companies, discovering issues and challenges that the buyer never reveals during an active sales situation. As marketers gain familiarity with each of the people involved in the buying decision, as well as the steps they take and the factors they evaluate, they can help sales anticipate the inevitable obstacles and prepare the tools and arguments that sales needs to move these decisions along. There's another outcome that is just as critical, though. When marketing and sales share the same understanding about the work that's required to win more business, the gap between the two organizations closes and they naturally become a more cohesive and effective team.

Resolving Ties between Your Company's Products and Those of the Competition

Companies that compete in mature markets experience intense price pressure as the differences between their products and their competitors' diminish and eventually disappear. Clever buyers are adept at playing one competitor against another as a negotiating tactic to secure the best price.

When you interview your buyers, you will learn that price is rarely the deciding factor in high-consideration buying decisions. You will come to understand how your buyers investigate and calculate the value/price equation, who is involved, and what your competitors are doing to create the perception that their solution is the best option. You will learn that other perceptions and concerns—especially those that are unfounded—often have a far greater impact on your buyers' decisions than you previously imagined. These insights will help you to devise relevant messaging strategies, new educational materials, or may even result in a new approach to your pricing models or product road map.

Identifying Which Types of Buyers You Need to Influence and How to Reach Them

Marketers know that they need to understand exactly who is involved in the buying decision and devise strategies to engage all of them. For example, sales and marketing professionals are often hearing that they need to reach the executives in their buyers' companies. Yet marketers have little clarity about the topics that will resonate with C-suite officers or the activities that they can undertake to engage them.

While recounting the story of their decision-making process, buyers will reveal to you who triggered the need to solve the problem and the steps the buyer and others took to evaluate their options. Buyers will describe how each of the influencers affected the choice of solutions at each stage in the selection process. They will describe any external factors that exerted an influence and the resources they relied upon to educate themselves about all of the options available to them. You'll have a chance to understand what they learned about each of the alternatives and how various sales and marketing activities affected their choices.

When you give your buyers a seat at the table, mastering these difficult marketing challenges—and more—becomes eminently possible. Buying Insights allow marketers to truly understand their buyers' mind-set and channel their voice at decisive internal meetings. Similarly, Buying Insights also provide guidance for marketing and salespeople to communicate effectively with their buyers.

Effective communication is essential in any mutually sustaining relationship. Building business relationships involves the exchange of ideas, information, products, and sometimes even ideals. The human exchange of communication between one entity and another informs and sustains all of our lives, and it's when we speak the same language, using words that limit unnecessary ambiguity and obfuscation, that it's possible to accomplish truly astounding things.

Buying Insight Opens Doors to C-Level Executives

Yes, the possibility to accomplish astounding things. Lest you suspect a bit of marketing hyperbole here, we'll end this chapter with a story that is both edifying and inspiring.

Maribeth Ross, Chief Content Officer at Aberdeen Group, provides the following true case study, which dramatically illustrates how creatively responding to Buying Insights can transform the sales experience and provide guidance to eliminate two major marketing challenges. When the marketing team at an actual company—here fictitiously referred to as COI—discovered their buyer persona's crucial Priority Initiatives and Perceived Barriers, they instituted an inspired program that got the attention of their buyer's C-level executives.

COI is an enterprise information and records management service company that works with organizations to facilitate the storage and retrieval of their proprietary documents and electronic records. According to Ross, the primary customer for COI's services had always been a relatively junior level person, a position known as a records manager. The records manager in most organizations is somewhat like a librarian: This is the person responsible for overseeing the cataloging and retention of important internal information and staying current on developments related to the field, including changing government and industry regulations and trends related to information storage.

In the past, COI had always marketed to the records manager based on this understanding of the position's role, sending detailed information about new regulations that they thought would be helpful.

When COI interviewed their records manager buyers, they discovered several surprising insights, which were captured in a buyer persona they called "Alicia." While the interviews confirmed Alicia's position was indeed librarian-like and ever-changing regulations were a concern, Alicia's biggest Perceived Barrier was, in fact, internal. In most organizations, Alicia wasn't accorded a strategically important management position and she didn't control budgets. Whenever new regulations went into effect, Alicia was responsible for educating the rest of the company about the new rules. However, implementing the required changes was extremely difficult because Alicia was unable to effectively engage the senior executives in her organization.

Seeing an opportunity to elevate Alicia's role as well as educate buyers about the many changing regulations that their solution addressed so that they could win more business, COI's marketing department implemented what was called a "Compliant Records Management Program." With this initiative, Alicia continued to learn about all the new regulations, but now COI also provided materials that were designed for Alicia to forward to upper-level offices—not only her boss, but to C-suite executives as well.

One of the most important tools the marketing team created was an assessment that identified the riskiest areas in corporate records management. COI's sales team had a compelling reason to meet with

Alicia and walk her through the survey questions. This created a great opportunity to educate Alicia about problems that she may have overlooked and qualify her as a prospect for additional COI services without the appearance of a sales pitch.

Even more valuable, however, was the follow-up report that COI sent to Alicia to tell her how her company compared to its peers. It was a relatively simple next step for Alicia to get a meeting with the executives once she had this tangible evidence of any shortcomings.

Within a few months, COI's sizable customer base had completed so many of these surveys that the company compiled the findings in an annual report of impressive authority. Within the industry, COI's report became recognized as the only one of its kind. It offered a clear overview about the state of records management across companies of all sizes, generating additional sales leads and enhancing COI's reputation as the industry leader. Each year thousands of records managers signed up for webinars when the report was unveiled. And for Alicia, it positioned the Compliant Records Management Program as an essential tool for doing her job more successfully.

The third and most valuable phase of this program occurred when COI's sales team was invited to discuss the results of the annual survey with their customers' senior executives. For the first time, COI salespeople had ready access to the executives who controlled the budget and a powerful tool to persuade them to invest in COI services. Not incidentally, these meetings allowed COI to reinforce the essential role played by Alicia, further cementing their partnership with the persona who was a key influencer in the selection of records management services.

COI's program worked because they focused on Alicia's Priority Initiative—a need to help her company respond to regulatory changes—and addressed her Perceived Barrier—an inability to be fully effective within her organization due to hierarchical constraints. COI's new resources not only helped their primary buyer persona, but also opened the doors to the C-suite executives who approved the budget for records management. By cleverly educating the C-level executives about the increasing importance of records managers throughout the business world, COI ensured that Alicia had the financial support to do her job while simultaneously solidifying their position as the leader in their field.

Is it any surprise that this program greatly expanded COI's base of customers and helped drive millions of additional dollars in revenue?

A truly astounding accomplishment. And a wonderful demonstration of what can happen when Buying Insights are astutely applied to marketing challenges.

3

Decide How You Will Discover Buyer Persona Insights

If, as Albert Camus wrote, "Life is the sum of all your choices," it is marketing's goal to better understand how those choices are made. Decoding and influencing decision making lies at the core of all marketing efforts.

Yet marketing is only one of several professions that want to know how people choose one option over another. Responding to the need, countless psychologists, neurologists, sociologists, and anthropologists have written books and papers that attempt to decode the "who, what, how, and why" of decision making in its many permutations. And now, as we walk through our days with increasingly Internet-connected devices, a new generation of data scientists is building complex algorithms that promise to glean meaningful insight from our digital footprints. It is dizzying to consider what all of these approaches might someday reveal or how future innovations will affect our lives.

Lacking a crystal ball and humbled by the potential for rapid change, we hope to simplify this topic, providing practical guidance that every marketer, regardless of budget, can employ to gain insights into their customer's buying decisions and the people who make them.

The Most Important Nine Months of My Career

We'll begin with the simple approach that I first learned in 1986 when I took a job as an account executive at Regis McKenna, the marketing consultancy and public relations (PR) firm that Apple, Intel, and most of the successful technology companies at that time trusted for their positioning and marketing strategies.

When I joined the firm at a small branch office in Phoenix, Regis McKenna, who gave his company his own name, had risen to prominence as one of Silicon Valley's new visionaries and had just published a book, *The Regis Touch: Million Dollar Advice from America's Top Marketing Consultant,* released in the months after the media frenzy surrounding the famous 1984 launch of Macintosh. (*Newsweek* referred to him as the "Silicon Valley Svengali.")

McKenna did not have a degree in marketing. Significantly, his liberal arts education included concentrated study in phenomenology, the niche area of philosophy that is largely devoted to the systematic study of subjective conscious experiences such as judgments, perceptions, and emotions. In his 1985 book, McKenna stressed the importance of continuous qualitative research: firsthand, broad-based study of competitors—their strengths and weaknesses—and the perceptions and attitudes of customers.

"Companies must satisfy customer needs, not simply produce goods," McKenna wrote in *The Regis Touch.* "And to do that, they must monitor and understand the environment." He then told a story of doing qualitative research in a retail store during the early 1970s when $100 and $200 pocket calculators were becoming a popular office item. He carefully watched a customer comparing two different models. From the way he was holding them in his hand, McKenna concluded that the customer was assessing their quality to some degree by their weight and heft. He saw the man purchase the heavier model and subsequently McKenna suggested to his client that they add extra weight to their calculators to give the perception that they were more substantial. The client did so and sales increased.

During my first week working for McKenna, I was assigned to learn how to conduct buyer interviews so that I could write the positioning for an upcoming Intel launch. Although I had worked in the technology industry for four years, there was nothing in my background that prepared me to talk about how this Intel technology would help telecommunications companies transmit digital data. I was astonished by how much I learned in the course of conducting these interviews, and the realization that I could obtain the clarity I needed to get the job done.

It would be years before I fully appreciated how much I learned during that first week on the job. The training I got at Regis McKenna never mentioned buyer personas. They trained me to conduct "internal and external audits," a terrible name for a great idea that involved interviewing internal stakeholders to understand their strategy, followed by buyer interviews to understand the buyers' point of view.

McKenna described the external audit process at the time: "We interview people from a number of different groups: existing customers, potential customers, distributors, industry 'experts,' financial analysts, and perhaps key journalists. We typically talk to a dozen or so people in all. . . . In these interviews we do not look for specific facts and figures. Usually, we do not even talk about the specific product. Rather we identify patterns, attitudes, and opinions that influence the thinking process."

I spent less than a year at Regis McKenna, and the approach that we now use to interview buyers has little in common with what I learned in that role. But those early buyer interviews gave me the confidence I needed to start my own consulting firm and, later, to accept senior executive positions running marketing and product management in three completely unrelated technology companies.

I had discovered the secret that would allow me to work almost anywhere: an ability to market even the most obscure technology to highly technical buyers by simply listening to what they had to say as they explained their perceptions about the decisions I wanted to influence. Once I could see where the buyer's needs intersected with our solutions, companies listened to me and paid me for my advice. I was hooked.

How Interviews Reveal Insight

There are many reasons that companies don't invest in market research, but chief among them is that companies have had bad experiences with methods that were not suited to answering their questions. It doesn't take too many reports that reveal nothing of interest before stakeholders conclude that market research doesn't work.

Expert marketers struggle right along with everyone else. David Ogilvy, the renowned advertising sage who reigned during the era depicted in the popular *Mad Men* TV series, memorably summarized the market research dilemma this way: "The trouble with market research is that people don't think how they feel, they don't say what they think, and they don't do what they say."

He's right. If you ask buyers to tell you what they think about a particular product or approach, you are unlikely to uncover anything that explains their choice. And because Ogilvy clients were advertising low-consideration products, it is easy to see he was frustrated. He was asking buyers to explain thinking that wasn't fully conscious when it occurred ("people don't think how they feel"), so he got justifications, not explanations ("they don't say what they think").

The reason that buyer interviews have been so valuable for us is that we started in the technology industry, where the buyers spend weeks, months, or years evaluating their options. We didn't realize it at the time, but this environment made it easy for us to create a methodology that was unknown in the research industry. As we conducted interview after interview, we saw that we could engage buyers in telling in-depth stories about these lengthy decisions. As we threw away the scripts and probed on the various aspects of their stories, we found that buyers would open up to us, revealing the trials, traumas, and triumphs of decisions that, had they gone awry, would have resulted in huge losses for their companies or personal reputations. We were amazed that the people we talked to didn't want the interview to end, and that when we finally concluded they often thanked us profusely, as if we had done them a favor.

As our clients heard what we had learned, they expressed amazement. In one workshop at a company that builds simulation software used by aerospace engineers, a product management executive was stunned as we replayed the interview we had recorded in advance of the training. This was our first-ever interview for this type of solution, yet she told us that she learned more in those 40 minutes than she had in her combined seven years in the company.

The interview methodology that is explained in detail in Part II of this book is unique. There is no other marketing research discipline that can compare with its ability to reveal insights about high-consideration buying decisions and the people who make them. Fortunately most people can learn this simple methodology, and because it focuses on a real story, the insights revealed during the course of building buyer personas are not subject to the "confirmation bias" that often occurs when research participants unconsciously provide answers they think the interviewer wants to hear.

Is This Another Kind of Qualitative Research?

In traditional market research, interviews are conducted as a part of a "qualitative" study. A critical first step with these qualitative interviews is the development of a carefully drafted "discussion guide." The researcher expends a considerable amount of time and effort to build a guidebook that reduces the risk that the wording or the order of the questions in the interview might affect the responses and accordingly skew the final research conclusions.

Marketers who have previously invested in traditional qualitative research are therefore surprised to learn that buyer persona research is best conducted using a structure and discipline that is uniquely different. We don't follow a script, we don't prepare questions in advance, and we avoid introducing new ideas during the interviews.

Our objective is to listen as real buyers tell their own stories—to capture the mind-set of buyers in the act of making the decision we want to influence. Fresh from the often harrowing experience of days, weeks, months, or perhaps even years dominated by the search for a solution to their problem, buyers can articulate exactly what triggered them to begin and, with the right prompting, reveal incredible details about what transpired as they cast a wide net for all available options before they ultimately chose one. In this construct, the researcher's role is that of a great listener, someone who is hanging on every word, encouraging buyers to reveal exactly what they saw, heard, and did as they determined which solutions to continue to evaluate, and which they decided to exclude.

In fact, as you will see in Chapter 5, only one question in this interview is scripted. This is the opening inquiry that takes buyers back to the first moment in their story, to the day when they first decided to look for a solution to their problem. As we follow this real-life story, we avoid the hypothetical inquiry that diverts the conversation into the realm of guesswork and speculation rather than an account of what actually happens. (In addition, hypotheticals are also far more likely to cause the respondent to try to give you the answer that they think you want to hear.)

So although it is accurate to say that the methodology in Part II is a form of qualitative research, you will want to carefully review that section to ensure that your interviews produce actionable Buying Insights.

Crafting the Low-Consideration Buyer's Story

If you are one of the fortunate marketers whose buyers invest considerable time evaluating their options, we urge you to read Part II to learn how these interviews can work for you. But as we explained in Chapter 1, marketers of products or services that involve little buyer consideration are unlikely to gain insights from this approach. The buyer who runs into a convenience store to buy a snack will not have much to say about that decision. And yet we know that there is a story here, and that marketers who understand that story are better equipped to influence their buyers' choices.

Jeffrey and Bryan Eisenberg, coauthors of *Buyer Legends: The Executive Storyteller's Guide,* explain it this way: "Stories place us in the hero's shoes and transfer subjective experience, just as if we ourselves had lived it. In stories, toys not only come to life, they can make us root for them, cry with them, and laugh with them. And so it is that Pixar can make an animated robot seem as real as the kid sitting next to us in the theater. Stories do far more than entertain. They are the context for how we connect with and understand each other. And they are a powerful means for transferring our experience to someone who hasn't lived it directly."

The Eisenberg brothers suggest that anyone can craft their buyer's story by writing a Buyer Legend. Their recommended approach begins with a single Buyer Profile and a team of internal stakeholders such as sales and customer service, ideally people who have some exposure to the needs of the buyer you want to influence.

In a team meeting, you ask everyone to imagine this buyer's decision and what might happen to prevent the buyer from achieving the destination you prefer. For example, what would a mother be thinking about as she shops for clothes for her children's first day of school? Does she visit your website or your retail store or both? Will she find it easy to discover the clothing that is good for school days? What concerns will she have about quality, size, and pricing?

Sometimes you will be guided by data from the internal or external sources that we will examine in the next few pages. In other cases your team will need to simply empathize with the buyer and brainstorm different steps the buyer might take, in much the same way that the agency marketers in Chapter 1 sat in Jessica's living room, thinking about the steps she would take to buy a car.

Considering that our personal experience has always involved listening to real buyer stories before we construct the narrative in the 5 Rings of Buying Insight, we understand that marketers might hesitate to build stories that are not grounded in reality. We hope that those of you who have very low-consideration solutions will not be discouraged. The chances are good that you could personally relate to the experience of buying a product like yours, and that a story like this can help you to spot gaps in your marketing or channel experiences.

Using B2B Salespeople to Build Buyer Personas

Business-to-business (B2B) marketers often ask us if they can rely on their sales representatives for insights into their buyer personas. This is a natural question because these reps have firsthand experience with buyers and can readily tell you which influencers impact the decision. Additionally, reps who are trained to be good listeners may help you to understand your buyer's concerns, needs, and goals. Many experienced salespeople have discovered that their attention to their buyer's perceptions, success indicators, and resistance points can result in a winning account strategy. As with low-consideration decisions, gathering this information from your salespeople can kick-start your efforts to understand a buyer's mind-set.

However, there are a number of reasons to cite caution. Salespeople are not in the habit of thinking about patterns in buyer behavior. The nature of sales engagement encourages salespeople to treat every account as unique, and any input they provide is likely to feature something about the few deals in which they are currently involved.

More important, salespeople witness a small slice of time in the Buyer's Journey, as buyers increasingly rely on their own sources to narrow their options before they are willing to meet with someone in sales. Therefore, your reps are unlikely to know anything about how the buyer navigated the earliest stages of the buying decision, a troubling limitation when this is the part of the buyer's decision that marketing needs to influence the most.

Furthermore, it's unlikely that salespeople can provide usable intelligence about the buyer's perceptions that negatively affect the outcome. The information conveyed to you from a sales representative who failed to close the deal provides a simplistic view of the situation; there are missing details that buyers won't reveal to sales reps out of fear that they will use these points to reengage with them.

Although it offers a possible starting point, relying on internal intelligence eliminates the possibility that you will learn anything new. If you market a solution that buyers consider at length, there remains a wealth of additional insight available to you.

The Pros and Cons of Buyer Surveys

Surveys are one of the most popular forms of market research. A relatively inexpensive and accessible methodology, these can quickly provide a quantitative statistical reading of predetermined questions and choices. The results are easy to report and establish a benchmark from which to measure future results. But because they cannot discover anything that is unexpected or unknown by the survey's designers, their findings are subject to unintended bias, which can be dangerous.

Surveys are of greatest value to buyer personas when they are used to validate the insights gained through other methodologies, especially in-depth interviews with small numbers of buyers. They are also used to identify buyer demographics, and the correlation of that information produces findings that can be helpful. For instance, survey results may suggest that in general married lawyers aged between 40 and 60 living in urban environments prefer Italy as a vacation destination rather than a location in the United States. If this result differs for younger or unmarried lawyers, or those in a different profession, this would suggest that travel industry marketers who have Italian vacation venues might want to target this Buyer Profile.

However, the survey method cannot reveal the Buying Insights that disclose the attorney's expectations while selecting from dozens of options regarding that vacation. Without these specifics, the travel agency marketers will know whom to target but remain guessing about how to position their remote villa as the ideal destination.

When to Use Focus Groups

Focus groups are another way to observe and understand people's choices, but this method delivers the most value when marketers have identified a number of alternative strategies and want to know which of them is most appealing to potential buyers.

The unique characteristic of focus group methodology lies in its ability to foster dialogue among a small group of participants and to use that conversation to build consensus or, in some instances, to observe closely as some of the participants split off into a separate group and argue for a competing perspective. Marketers listen closely through two-way mirrors, online cameras, or recordings, watching for the physical and verbal cues that determine whether Campaign A or B is the best option for their launch plan.

The principal weakness of focus groups for buyer personas is that any form of "group think" distorts the individual perspective, as people's voices are quieted by a desire for harmony, conformity, or conflict avoidance. And due to their cost there is little reason to recommend their use for buyer persona development. It is far better to reserve focus groups for their best use—evaluating and contrasting your buyers' reactions to variations of your marketing tactics.

Will Big Data Deliver Insights?

Perhaps it was inevitable. The global spread of digital technologies, communications, commerce, mobile smartphones, and social media has given rise to the collection of massive amounts of information. It didn't take long for the providers of pioneering Internet sites that were selling books, music, and consumer items to realize the great value contained in the information about each online transaction. As a result, as early as the mid-1990s it was possible to encounter online promotions suggesting products geared to your recent purchases.

Now every retail business wants in on this action. Grocery stores that offer generous discounts for using their "loyalty card" aren't thanking you for your business. They are collecting reams of data about your purchase history and using it to guide decisions about how to win more of your business.

Two decades later, the collection of massive quantities of data about nearly every living person on the planet is ushering in marketing's new frontier. The anonymous demographic information revealed in consumer surveys of the recent past is paltry compared to the myriad intelligence currently in the hands of commercial data brokers. The practice of onboarding—the merging of data collected from multiple sites with specific identifying information—has created detailed, individual digital marketing dossiers. In 2014, Acxiom, one the largest of these data brokers, claimed to have more than 3,000 data points on every adult American. Journalists have reported that these range from telephone numbers and financial information to religious preferences—including whether one reads the Bible regularly—and political affiliation. It even includes detailed medical information. Purchases, whether online or in stores, are recorded. So are movies watched, repeated words and phrases that occur in emails, and the relevant phrases highlighted in a personal e-book reader. And, as is now widely acknowledged, smartphones routinely transmit their location via GPS apps, only adding to the accumulating information on every user's activities.

The implications for marketing are huge. Besides categorizing interests and predicting possible future purchases based on a correlation with others of the same profile, there is great potential to understand some of the mysterious factors that affect low-consideration purchasing decisions.

One segment of the data collection industry is even concentrating on gathering data about the real-time emotional state of online users. For example, a data analytics company, Argus Labs, has created software for smartphones designed to chart a user's emotions throughout the day based on the data collected by the phone. Since medical monitoring applications are already being used on a number of smartphones and other wearable personal mobile devices, Argus's application or others like it may soon be commonplace.

At Facebook, a psychological experiment conducted in early 2012 provided altered news feeds to 700,000 of its users to determine whether their emotions would be affected by the manipulated content. The published study reported that the unwitting subjects of the Facebook experiment did indeed appear to be emotionally affected by the altered content based upon the words used in subsequent communications. There is little doubt that Argus, Facebook, and other data collection firms are well aware of the lucrative marketing possibilities available should information on personal emotional states become an easily accessible data point.

Whether Buying Insights can be developed from big data remains unproven, but this expanding frontier suggests intriguing as well as unsettling possibilities as we enter a new era of demographics on steroids. Will it be possible to discern clues into the subconscious realms of impulse decision making by employing algorithm correlations from data about emotions, location, and demographics? Or are we to discover that impulse decisions are far more mysterious than even this accumulation of big data will reveal?

But one thing appears certain in the years to come. Big data intelligence processing will be part of our lives whether we like it or not. And for marketers accessing this intelligence there are bound to be periods of adjustments as the parameters are refined for accuracy.

It's also worth pointing out that despite the wealth of data being collected, the results are subject to a classic statistical dilemma: Just because there is a correlation in data doesn't prove the causation. A subscription to *Brides* magazine may be a very a good predictor that the subscriber is planning a marriage. But stopping the subscription doesn't mean the wedding will be canceled any more than changing the subscription to *Yachting* is a good predictor that the wedding will now take place on a boat. This example may seem ludicrous, but it illustrates a common fallacy that predictive data reveals the underlying cause behind it (i.e., people plan weddings because they subscribe to *Brides*).

There is an equally significant caveat that comes with big data. As an oft-repeated aphorism says, "With great power comes great responsibility." I know a writer with a young family who had a rude awakening to the implications of personal data mining a few years ago. He had been given a grave diagnosis of stage IV cancer and had shared his thoughts about his condition with a small circle of friends via email. Although he was fairly open about his feelings in those private emails, he was startled when a political article on the *Washington Post*'s website was accompanied by a display ad showing a teenage girl crying over a tombstone inscribed "Daddy." The headline read, "Who will look after her when you are gone?" The insurance company ad was crafted to appeal directly to this writer's buyer persona, but you can imagine his shock that this apparently private exchange was somehow known to the advertiser.

The story has a happy ending: The writer is now in full recovery and doctors see no indication of the cancer's return. What didn't recover was his expectation that personal information related in emails, Internet searches, or via private messages was, in fact, private. My friend did not reason that the ad placement was simply a coincidence, but he also didn't imagine that anyone was personally reading his email. Instead, he concluded that the frequency of the word "cancer" in his email and related online searches triggered a tag linked to his computer ID and demographic profile (which likely included his age, financial background, insurance history, and the fact that he is father of two young children, one of whom is female) and delivered the ad directly to his personal computer.

Creepy or just downright dumb? Overtly targeted ads that betray unexpected big data surveillance tend to backfire as they call more attention to their intrusive methodology than to successfully pitching the product or service being advertised. But as these methods become commonplace and accepted, much more subtle approaches are likely to replace clumsy attempts like the one just described.

How Social Media Contributes to Buyer Personas

Is your buyer on Twitter, Facebook, LinkedIn, Pinterest, or any of the other many social networks? If the answer is yes, your next question is whether the buyer is doing anything through that social network that helps you understand how he or she makes the decision you want to influence.

As the use of social media is changing rapidly, we can't answer this question for you. However, the nature of social media means that it is easy for you to join each of these networks and find the answer for yourself. Want to know if your buyer is on Twitter? Join yourself and use any of a dozen tools to monitor activity for keywords related to your solution or category. Most customer service organizations are already taking this step, so they may also be able to provide this data for you.

B2B marketers can gain great insight into their Buyer's Profile through online communities such as LinkedIn. Even if you are not "connected" to these people, many will make their profiles open for anyone to read. We often visit the LinkedIn pages of the people we interview to understand their job description and education. This eliminates the need to ask people obvious questions during our interviews and allows us to devote the entire time to hearing their stories. We also find that a search for recruiting ads can help us to understand the skills and experience that are most valued by our buyer's boss.

B2B marketers will also find it valuable to monitor discussion groups on LinkedIn and other professional sites to see which topics are generating the most engagement, and to hear how people describe their concerns and opinions. Although these sources are unlikely to reveal Buying Insights, you may find links to blogs, product reviews, articles, interviews, and white papers that your buyers are interested in reading. If you see a lot of engagement in any of these places, you will want to note that in your Buyer Profile.

SAP Gains High-Value Insights through Web Analytics

We have noticed that there is a huge gap between the value that marketers of low- and high-consideration products derive from Web analytics. For those in the low-consideration category, the fact that the website experience captures so much of the buying decision has triggered huge investments in tools that analyze and adjust the buyer's interaction on the Web in order to facilitate increased sales. But marketers of high-consideration solutions, whose buyers are offline during most of the buying experience, tend to the opposite extreme, almost ignoring the digital trail left by their buyers.

In one notable exception, Michael Brenner, who was then a vice president of marketing at SAP, a global software company, wanted to understand which stage of the Buyer's Journey his buyers were in when they visited the company's website. The answer was quickly revealed when he saw that 99.97 percent of the visitors to SAP.com had used product or brand-specific search terms to enter the site.

Concerned, Brenner decided to look at Web traffic for one of the company's strategic solutions. A quick check on Google told him that millions of people a month were searching on "what is Big Data?" Brenner didn't need to interview anyone to know that these were people he wanted to educate about the SAP approach. And when he compared those Google search results to the 13 people who had asked "what is SAP Big Data," he didn't need a data scientist to tell him that only three in 10,000 people were finding SAP's answer to this question.

We decided to end this chapter with Brenner's story because it reveals that simple inquiries can result in big insights. We have undoubtedly missed many of the options you might take to learn about your buyers, and encourage you to use the approach that reveals as much as insight as possible. Unfortunately, most marketers have never considered the possibility that anything other than intuitive guesswork is even possible. And for many business-to-consumer marketers, this is mostly true. Marketers of low-consideration products may have to satisfy themselves with limited data about how, when, and why buyers make the decisions they want to influence.

But B2B marketers of medium- to high-consideration solutions have a clear and unique opportunity to engage their buyers, asking them questions, detailing their stories, and capturing their language. We have the opportunity to listen before we speak.

PART

II

Interviewing for Buying Insights

"Go to the source. Get their story in their own words."

It's the advice that any news editor would tell a fledging journalist faced with the task of discovering the facts about something or someone they've been assigned to cover.

A writer asked to compose an in-depth profile about a filmmaker, author, business leader, or politician is likely to talk to the friends, family, and associates of the subject, but would be remiss if he or she didn't try to interview the central character of the article as well.

As you consider your options for conducting buyer interviews, it is helpful to think about the characteristics of a good journalist. The people who excel are innately curious, good listeners, and open to the challenges of an unscripted conversation with people they don't know.

Recall an interview by a great journalist and you may recall that it seemed like you were listening to a private conversation. Even if the journalist was interviewing a head of state, the interviewer was comfortable with a conversational dialog, effortlessly prompting for the next part of a fascinating story. When an answer was incomplete, the journalist took a slightly different tack with a follow-up question, persisting in uncovering the details that revealed the leader's mind-set. As the story unfolded, you were privileged to gain insight into a high-stakes situation and decision that you will never personally encounter.

Many people will not want to master this type of interview. But there are thousands of successful journalists who are not Barbara Walters. We hope that these next few chapters will help you understand the methodology that leads buyers to reveal the insights you need. Some of you will feel compelled to pick up the phone, others will want more training, and many will know that this is a job best left to others.

After all, how many of us can sing in tune? Practice and experience certainly make a huge difference, but many of us are unlikely to be offered a recording contract no matter how much we practice.

Timing is another dimension of the decision to do this work yourself. If results are needed immediately an outside research firm is likely to produce completed buyer personas within six to eight weeks, while buyer interviewing and analysis conducted internally will likely compete with in-house marketing projects and may take longer to complete.

On the other hand, although experienced interviewers are most likely to cover all relevant aspects of the inquiry in the allotted time, marketers who know their business intimately may guide their interviews into unexpected areas of discovery, gaining insights that lead to the new product ideas that we will discuss in Chapter 11.

Whether you choose to buy them or build them, you should know as much as you can about the methodology behind interviewing high-consideration buyers for Buying Insights. We hope that every marketer will use these upcoming chapters to understand how insight is discovered, analyzed, and presented for actionable buyer personas.

In Part II, Chapter 4 provides tips for those of you who might need to convince your company that interviews are necessary. Then we'll show you how to choose the people you want to interview and how to approach them and secure permission for the meeting. Chapter 5 details the unique methodology for conducting effective buyer interviews and recommended ways to ask probing questions to reveal deeper insight. Once you have conducted your interviews, Chapter 6 shows you how your intelligence should be processed, organized, and analyzed in a format that helps you classify the most important information and discern where each pertinent gem of knowledge belongs in the persona's Buying Insights. Finally, Chapter 7 tackles one of the thorniest and most important questions you are likely to face when processing your data: determining how many buyer personas you will need.

4

Gain Permission and Schedule Buyer Interviews

As much as we may like to think of ourselves as open-minded, most people's initial response to a new idea is resistance. And yet it is difficult to imagine how our lives would be affected if change was not only permitted but encouraged.

> The abolishment of pain in surgery is a chimera. Knife and pain are two words in surgery that must forever be associated in the consciousness of the patient.
> —*Dr. Alfred Velpeau, French surgeon in 1839*
>
> This "telephone" has too many shortcomings to be seriously considered as a practical form of communication.
> —*Western Union internal memo, 1878*
>
> There is no reason for any individual to have a computer in their home.
> —*Kenneth Olsen, president and founder of Digital Equipment Corp.*

Although your goal to interview your buyers doesn't register on this scale, we know that many marketers encounter skepticism or outright resistance to their plans to contact buyers and hear their stories.

It's interesting to note that the resistance you are most likely to experience will come from your internal stakeholders and that many buyers will respond positively to your request to interview them. There are exceptions, of course, but despite the logical and relatively economical ideas in this book, it's not unusual to hear these reactions from stakeholders when marketers introduce the need for buyer personas:

"Show me proof of the ROI."

"We already know our buyers. Why should we pay for unnecessary qualitative research?"

"Our customers are unique. Broad generalizations can't capture the thinking of individuals."

"If I'm going to invest money in marketing, I want more leads, not research."

Maybe you've heard these arguments before. Although resistance can be dispiriting, it's not that difficult to construct a persuasive case for interviewing your buyers to understand their mind-set. And industry trends are on your side as more and more organizations are persuaded of the great potential of buyer persona insight.

Persuade Stakeholders That You Need Buying Insights

If you encounter resistance to building buyer personas, you will want to focus on the result and not the concept itself. No one outside of marketing wants to hear about a new approach to marketing. Try to sell the idea of buyer personas and you may trigger a story about what happened the last time someone came in with a bright idea that was going to solve everything. Frankly, trying to sell buyer personas to internal audiences is a lot like promoting your products to buyers who aren't looking for them.

Now is the time to think about your internal stakeholders' persona. You may already know about a key priority that requires effective marketing, or you may need to interview stakeholders to clarify the outcomes that are most important to them. With these goals in view, suggest how a goal of particular importance can be achieved—not by emphasizing marketing research methods, but by calling attention to the way Buying Insight will help you to understand the customer expectations and concerns that your marketing needs to address.

For example, if there is a need to fill the sales pipeline with more qualified leads, talk about how you want to understand what motivates buyers to consider solutions like yours, plus the perceptions that cause buyers to maintain the status quo. If your company has a plan to introduce a new product, focus on the need to know how various buyers will respond to the new solution while helping salespeople to strategize ways to overcome their objections.

Ideally, your first buyer persona should address an initiative that is critical and where everyone agrees success cannot readily be achieved by doing business as usual. The criticality will help you assign internal resources or the budget you need to conduct the buyer interviews. And because the outcome isn't guaranteed, your internal stakeholders will be more willing to adjust their strategies based on what you learn.

By taking on this crucial project, you are diverting your stakeholders' attention away from the Buyer Persona tool and training the spotlight on what is profoundly meaningful to them: their own Priority Initiatives, Success Factors, and Perceived Barriers.

Overcome the "We Know Our Buyers" Objection

Companies tend to start out with a fairly clear picture of their buyers. Entrepreneurs are usually prompted to start a company when a personal experience reveals a need that isn't being met. For a while, their intimate knowledge of that problem fuels the small team they build to bring the solution to market. Everyone is invigorated by that vision, and although the company remains relatively small, it is likely that each member of the team has regular contact with customers. But as successful enterprises grow, their employees begin to specialize. Gradually yet inevitably, internal dynamics begin to impact decisions. Marketers, in particular, are likely to be cut off from the customer interactions that would help them to understand their buyers and what affects their decisions.

If the founding executives are currently leading your company, they may not understand why you feel the need to interview your buyers. Or they may direct you to the sales teams who meet almost daily with buyers to understand their concerns and win those deals. In fact, there is no denying that salespeople know more than anyone else about the buyers in their individual accounts.

Should you hear that the company's internal knowledge of buyers is sufficient, it is best to avoid resistance. Instead work toward finding common ground. If your stakeholder says, "Research is unnecessary; we already know our buyers," begin by accepting their offer to share their expertise.

"That's wonderful," you should tell the stakeholder. "This may save us a lot of work."

Follow this by setting a time for a meeting where you can learn as much as possible about the buyers. Explain that you will conduct a mock buyer persona interview, in which the stakeholder will role-play the part of the buyer.

Not surprisingly, any such interview will be prone to some bias, and the insights are highly unlikely to be representative of the market as a whole. But it's also possible that the stakeholder knows the organization's buyers well and can be helpful to you.

You will want to conduct the interview using the guidelines that you will learn in Chapter 5. During the mock interview, watch for any holes in the story or look for moments when the stakeholder begins to veer into a sales pitch rather than channeling an authentic buyer's voice. For example, someone who is accurately role-playing a buyer would have a balanced perspective of your solution. If your buyer-expert gives a response that sounds as if he is reading your marketing collateral, you need to call him on it. "Hold on, John," you should interject. "Are you sure you are actually staying in role here? This sounds awfully optimistic. If all the buyers think the way you've been speaking to me right now, why aren't we winning every deal?"

As the meeting continues, ask the stakeholder to next take on the role of a buyer who failed to buy your solution. This exercise will reveal the degree to which the stakeholder is aware of buyer criticism and the barriers that are hindering sales. Don't be surprised if the sales expert tells you that buyers are choosing others because your solution is too expensive. You'll want to respond by saying, "That's interesting, because we know that people choose solutions based on value, not price. Can you tell me what the buyer thinks about the fact that we can do [unique capability]? What do you think we would need to do to explain how our solution delivers enough value to justify the premium price?"

Stakeholders who encountered difficulty answering your questions objectively will now realize that there are aspects to the buyers' mind-set they don't know. A better appreciation of the insight the buyer persona methodology can reveal should make them far more receptive.

When You Don't Have Time for Buyer Persona Interviews

It will come as no surprise that most stakeholders are focused on the immediate. Engaging in marketing research is often perceived as an unnecessary diversion of valuable time and resources. You might hear something like this: "What we really need are new leads. I certainly don't have the time to engage in a huge study. We need deliverables, and we need to get everything in gear as soon as possible."

When resistance like this is offered as an argument against engaging in buyer persona research, it is time to look for common ground. First, diminish any ideas about the magnitude of the project by stating emphatically that what you are proposing is not a massive study involving scores of interviews. Next, focus on the specific Buying Insights that you need before you can succeed with the goal that is an urgent priority.

As before, a mock interview in which the stakeholder plays the role of a buyer is an effective way to convey what it's possible to discover through buyer interviews. When you point out that these insights can be gleaned from a relatively small number of interviews, ask the stakeholder to compare this with the time and resources recently expended in other lead finding attempts. Viewed as a simple ROI analysis, the time and effort to conduct buyer interviews is minimal. Be sure to reinforce your goal to focus on the buyer interviews that will support this high-priority goal, reassuring your stakeholder that you do not plan to build buyer personas for everyone involved in every decision your solutions address.

Keep the focus on the Buying Insights you need to achieve a high-priority goal, use your insights to achieve an amazing result, and it won't be long before the tables are turned, with your stakeholders asking you if you've interviewed the buyers who are the target of an upcoming initiative. Won't that be nice?

Use Your Sales Database to Find Buyers to Interview

You will ideally want to create an alliance with sales as you prepare to interview your buyers. Because your interviews will focus on recent evaluators of solutions like yours, the sales organization should have a database that includes the names, phone numbers, and email addresses of many of the people you will want interview. We will soon talk about other ways to find buyers to interview, but sales is one resource that you will want to explore, especially if you plan to do your own interviews rather than outsourcing them to a third party.

We recommend that your head of marketing initiate this request with the head of sales and that you do not take your request directly to a sales representative. Remember that your initiative will be entirely new and unexpected, and that sales will naturally be protective of their relationships with customers and prospects.

We have found that it's helpful for your senior marketing executive to observe that while salespeople are trained to listen to their buyers' needs, goals, and concerns as a foundation for any presentation or proposal, marketing has traditionally worked with little or no insight into the needs of the buyers they hope to influence. Couple this with the fact that it's more difficult to persuade markets full of buyers (the marketer's job) rather than one buyer at a time (the purview of sales) and it's easy to see that marketing has a compelling reason to rectify this situation.

Now the conversation between your executives can focus on your department's desire to build more qualified leads and persuasive market-ing messages, programs, and sales tools, and how those are guided by insights into your buyer's expectations. Who could argue with this logic?

Sometimes You Want to Avoid Your Internal Database

In a perfect world, your sales management would be receptive to your marketing executive's request, your sales database would provide accu-rate names and contact information for the buyers who influence the outcome of your deals, and you would know exactly when the decision had been finalized so that you could contact those buyers to request an interview.

But even when sales is cooperative, you may want to use other resources to find at least some of the buyers you will interview. The first reason is that these databases, in our experience, are not as clean as we would hope. We've seen lists where less than 10 percent of the information is accurate, creating nothing but frustration for everyone involved.

In addition, your need for buyer interviews may intersect with the activities of others within your organization. Perhaps these buyers will be the subject of interviews for a sales department win/loss analysis or a marketing success story. You won't want to have several contacting the same person for different versions of the buyer's story, and unfortunately, the option to combine your objectives with these others isn't feasible. An interview for a win/loss analysis follows a highly scripted format intended to examine and illuminate a sales organization's successes and failures. (Conventionally, either sales operations or a third-party provider conducts the interview with the buyer.) As you will learn in Chapter 5, win/loss interviews address a very different set of objectives and follow a very different pattern than the interviews you need to conduct.

Similarly, buyers interviewed for a success story tell only a selected portion of the narrative and relate it with awareness that their account will be used for a promotional press release. Their story may illuminate the reasons behind their decision, as well as details about the implementation and any associated benefits, but once again the interview does not lend itself to full disclosure of Buying Insights.

Should you become aware that the buyers you plan to contact for buyer persona interviews have already been subjected to a win/loss inquiry or asked for a success story, you will want to forego the request for an additional interview.

Using Professional Recruiters to Set Interview Appointments

A quick search on the Internet for "qualitative research recruiters" will turn up thousands of agencies that specialize in finding the people you want to interview. For a fee that is typically between $150 and

$200 per interview, these recruiting companies will work with your specifications to locate buyers much like yours and set up appointments for your interviews. In addition to the agency fee, you will be asked to pay each participant an "incentive fee" that ranges from $100 to $300 for a 30-minute phone interview.

Should you have a budget, there are several obvious reasons why these services are an attractive option. First, you can skip the need to consult with sales and stop thinking about the quality of your database or its overlap with the needs of your other internal stakeholders. Second, you that you can avoid the steps we will cover later in this chapter to persuade buyers to talk to you.

However, the most valuable reason to work with a recruiting service is that you can interview buyers who have never considered your solution. Should you want to enter a new market, launch a new product, or simply want to understand what's causing buyers to exclude your company from consideration, these recruiting resources are essential.

To work with these companies, you will want to build a "screener" that they can use to find buyers who are qualified for your buyer persona study. This is accomplished by working with your internal stakeholders to define the demographics for your typical buyer, which may include any or all of the following:

- Job titles
- Company size
- Industries
- Geographic location

In addition, you will want the recruiter to screen the participants to ensure that they have recently completed the evaluation of a solution like yours. This question should appear on the screener with these words: "Have you, within the last six months, participated in the evaluation of a [your solution category]?"

If your solution category is new or difficult to define, you can write this question a bit differently: "Have you, within the past six months, evaluated one or more of the following solutions?" Then list the names of the products that your buyer would have evaluated to solve the same problem that your product will address.

You will need to give the recruiter access to a public version of your calendar or blocks of time that you will hold open for these interviews. Then sit back, relax, and wait for the appointments to appear.

Which Buyer Should You Interview?

In virtually any high-consideration buying decision, whether business-to-business (B2B) or business-to-consumer (B2C), multiple people will be involved in the outcome and you will need to decide which of them you will interview. The preferred way to make this choice is to think about which of the buyers is "doing the work" to evaluate the various options and make a recommendation to the others who are involved in the decision. This person will have the most insight into the solutions that were evaluated and why one ultimately prevailed over all others.

Marketers of high-consideration B2B solutions tend to adopt the sales organization's lingo and equate their buyer persona with the "decision maker," generally the person who controls the budget. Since sales has to gain final approval from this individual to close the business, they want to focus on this person, who we'll refer to as the economic buyer.

Step into the marketing organization, however, and we can see the necessity to persuade each of the people who influence the buying decision. In a very high-consideration technology buying decision, for example, we might see an economic buyer, a technical buyer, and possibly several other buying influencers who represent the interests of the different groups of users. In Chapter 7 we'll talk about whether you need to build buyer personas for each of these different influencers (you'll be surprised at the answer), but for now let's keep the focus on which of these buying influencers you want to interview.

Although marketers expect that they should go straight to the economic buyer—the "decision maker"—this person is unlikely to have participated in each of the steps of the evaluation and can tell you only part of what you want to discover for the 5 Rings of Buying Insight. The economic buyer is likely to have triggered the decision to solve the problem and then handed off the nuts and bolts of the evaluation to someone else. Let's call this person the technical buyer. This person may or may not work in the technology department, but we use this label to define the person who examines all of the technicalities of the decision, interfacing with all stakeholders and managing the extended assessment that characterizes high-consideration decisions.

The more senior the buyer, the less likely that person will be able to provide important details about how the final outcome came to pass. Add to this the difficulty of scheduling any extended time with senior C-suite level executives, and you can see why we don't often recommend that you interview the economic buyer.

The buyer you will generally want to interview was interfacing with your sales team (as well as your competitor's representatives) and is thus easily identified. Because this person was overseeing the entire evaluation and working with each of the stakeholders, he or she can give you valuable information about all of the others who played a role in influencing the eventual outcome. If you want to identify this buyer for a new product, you will want to work with the recruiters described earlier, asking them to help you find the person who is most involved in weighing various options and recommending the best one.

Even if several different types of buyers are involved in the decision you want to influence, there is a point of diminishing return if you attempt to conduct interviews with all of them. There are exceptions, and if you have the resources to conduct additional interviews, there is no reason not to proceed. However, the information you gather in that single interview is the most cost-effective way to discover Buying Insights.

Interview Buyers Who Chose You as Well as Those Who Did Not

As you contemplate the universe of buyers who can relate the story about their decision, you can see that they logically fall into the following four categories:

1. People who considered you and chose you (your customers)
2. People who considered you but chose a competitor
3. People who considered you but decided to keep things as they were, to maintain the status quo
4. People who never considered you and chose another (either they chose a direct competitor, or if your solution is a new innovation, they chose a different way to solve the problem)

Before we talk about these, let's consider a fifth category of people: buyers who are currently considering your solution. As active sales prospects, these are people whom you should not interview until the decision is complete. Although it's unlikely that anything you might say would influence your buyer's decision, it's important that your salespeople maintain exclusive control over these interactions.

This restriction might appear to create a dilemma, especially for companies with a large installed base of customers. Inevitably, the sales organization is continuously working to sell new solutions into its established base, and marketers might conclude that this prevents them from interviewing any of those customers. This is untrue, however, and you can see why if you remember that we want to interview people about a decision that they have recently completed. Now you only need to ensure that this particular decision has concluded before the buyer is eligible for an interview.

Of the buyers who are available to interview, Group B—those who considered you but chose another—consistently yields the most valuable data, as they can articulate how and why they arrived at the conclusion that your solution was not as valuable as someone else's. In other words, they can tell us where things went wrong.

Surprisingly, buyers who chose a competitor are not only the most useful buyers to interview but also among the most amenable to speaking with you. Most marketers suspect that potential buyers whom you lost to a competitor wouldn't want to waste time on an interview. In fact, the opposite is true—these buyers are usually the most willing to tell you what happened. They've invested a good deal of time considering your approach, and would not have done so if they didn't believe that you had potential. Having determined that something about your company or solution is insufficient, these buyers often experience strong feelings, something akin to a personal relationship that ended badly, and are anxious to tell the whole, often colorful, story.

Even though buyers who didn't choose you are among the most likely to agree to an interview and provide the most valuable data, unfortunately they are also the most difficult to locate. The reason: The sales department is usually reluctant to forward information about deals they have lost.

The easiest interviews to arrange are those with buyers who selected you—those who have recently determined that your solution is an exact match for their needs. However, you will want to avoid too much focus on this category of buyers, because their story reflects only situations in which your organization got it right, at least for the most part. You wouldn't want to exclude these buyers from the interviews either, as they can tell you which aspects of your sales and marketing interactions are most important to them. You'll want to report this positive news to ensure the ongoing investment in the highest-impact activities.

The third category, Group C—people who started and then stopped considering your solution—are fairly easy to locate. Marketing is likely to have a database that includes the names and contact information of people who attended a webinar, left contact information at a trade show, or downloaded a white paper. Alas, these people are among the least likely to interview with you. They've invested relatively little time with you during the decision-making process and are therefore relatively unlikely to spend time talking about it. The trick with this group is finding a reason for them to speak with you. We've seen marketers post signs at trade shows announcing, "$50 to Pick Your Brain" in an attempt to gather insight from buyers in this category, and they had more volunteers than they could manage. Naturally, members of Group C are only going to be able to tell you about the initial stages of the buying and evaluation process. If you focus too much on these buyers, you will miss many of the Buying Insights that you need.

Contacting Buyers to Request an Interview

With a preliminary list of contacts in hand, it's now time to start reaching out and making contact with your potential interviewees.

Ideally you want to work with buyers who have made their buying decision within the last three to six months. Doing so will ensure that the buyer recalls vividly many aspects of the decision-making process and can impart as much detail as possible for your research. You will also want to interview people before they start to implement the solution, if that's possible. (The implementation experience can quickly overshadow the buying experience; if they are already using the product, they are more likely to want to talk about implementation aspects.) It's certainly possible to interview buyers as much as a year after the decision, but your buyer will be able to recall many more details if you conduct the inquiry shortly after the evaluation process.

The allotted time for the interview should be roughly 20 to 30 minutes. For a medium-consideration decision—one in which the buyer allotted a few days or a week or more during the evaluation—this is about the right amount of time. For decisions that required months or even years to conduct the full evaluation, you can ask for 30 minutes, but that's the maximum amount of time to request, even though the conversation may eventually run far longer.

Sending an email might seem the logical best way to approach a buyer for an interview; however, it's not suggested when making the first contact. Nearly everyone today finds managing their email a chore, and inbox messages from unfamiliar names are often left unopened in a rush to attend to urgent notes from known contacts.

Instead, placing a phone call is a far more effective strategy. Chances are your first phone call will land you in a voice mail box, but its purpose is to leave a message so that the person you want to interview will be more likely to open your email. By calling first and leaving the right kind of voice mail message, they are far more likely to read your follow-up email and consider your request.

A voice mail also allows you an opportunity to use a tone of voice that convinces your buyer that you are someone who will be interesting to talk to. Naturally, you should sound both professional and appreciative of their time. You might want to record yourself leaving this message and then play it back while attentively listening to make sure you don't sound in any way apologetic. If you feel guilty for interrupting their time and making the request, it will be conveyed in your tone of voice and give your buyer a reason to discount the importance of your inquiry. I realize that you may in fact feel guilty about asking this important person to schedule time with you, but as you gain experience with the interviews, you'll discover that buyers actually enjoy engaging in this kind of conversation, and many will want to talk at some length, keeping you on the phone far past the time you have allotted.

In your message, be completely transparent about the purpose of your call. It's a good idea to practice your opening until you can confidently explain the purpose of your call without stumbling.

When you make your call to request an interview, you'll confront one of three possibilities. You'll either connect to voice mail, get an administrative assistant, or you'll actually speak to the buyer on the phone. As most people have caller ID, you'll want to use your office phone so your company name shows up. About 95 percent of the time you will be connected to voice mail; however, if you call just before the working day begins or at the conclusion of the day in the time zone of your buyer, it's just possible you may reach a buyer who's catching up on work.

Here is a sample of what your voice mail message should say; however, it's advisable not to follow a script as reading from one often makes the message sound artificial:

My name is _____, and I'm in the marketing organization with [your organization]. I'm calling because you recently evaluated our [specific product or service], and I'm hoping that I can get a few minutes to talk with you about your experience as you went through that evaluation.

This isn't a survey; I'm looking for your candid feedback about what worked and what didn't as you went through that process. I'm hoping I can get about a 20-minute time slot in your calendar within the next week. Here's my phone number: [phone number]. I realize that it may be easier for you to respond to me via an email, so I'm going to follow up right now with an email, and definitely look forward to hearing back from you and hope we can talk soon.

If you connect with an administrative assistant, the odds of getting the interview actually increase. You give the same introductory request; however, since you are speaking to an actual person you also have an opportunity to uncover any objections, explain the purpose of your call, and enroll the assistant's help getting the interview. If the assistant is on your side, he or she will help you get to the boss. It's a good idea to use first names, "Tina, I would like to talk to Susan about . . ." And include your title if it helps. (If your title doesn't carry much weight because you are trying to reach someone in a much higher position, leave it out.) Again, the tone of your voice is important. Speak in the same tone as you would to a peer.

Immediately after leaving your voice mail message or talking with an administrative assistant, you should follow up with an email. Here is a sample:

> **Subject:** Re: _____ Interview
> Hi _____,
> I left a voice mail a few minutes ago but thought it might be more convenient for you to respond to an email.
> This absolutely isn't a sales call. I'm interviewing people who have recently evaluated our [category of solution], looking for insights into how we're supporting the market's buying process. We want to hear your candid thoughts about what worked well for you as well as areas for improvement.
> Please note that no salesperson will be on the call and this isn't a survey. Your thoughts will be used to improve the buying experience for you and others in your role.
> If you're willing to help me out with a 20- to 30-minute conversation, please suggest a time between Friday, October 16, and Friday, October 30. I'm in the time zone and am available starting at 7:30 a.m.
> Best regards, _____
> (Phone number)

If you get no response, you may wonder how many times you should call back and make another request for an interview. If you don't get a response, it's best to move on. If, on the other hand, you have a very short list of contact names, then you'll have to persist in trying to make contact as well as reach out to others on your short list. When making a second attempt, don't leave another voice mail. Instead try to try to reach the buyer at the times when they are likely to be in their office. After you've sent an email and left a voice mail, the buyer may pick up the phone, as he now knows who you are and why you're calling. If need be, call another two or three times, hoping to catch the buyer and avoid another message. But if you can't make contact after those attempts, move on to other names.

Now that you know how to find buyers to interview, we'll explore the methodology for conducting those interviews. Prepare to be amazed at how readily the phone meetings you have just scheduled will expose the surprising, factual, and useful insights that guide effective marketing decisions.

5 | Conduct Probing Buyer Interviews

Situational clichés in magazine cartoons never seem to go out of date. There's the deserted island with the single palm tree, the new arrival greeting St. Peter at the gates of heaven, and the corporate boardroom meeting with the gigantic chart indicating rapidly declining sales.

Then there's the seeker of truth climbing a lofty mountain to obtain enlightenment from a lone ascetic hermit. Underlying that situational cliché is the viewer's acceptance that all wisdom comes from asking the right person the right questions.

Perhaps not as challenging as scaling one of those cartoon mountains, learning the technique of conducting effective buyer persona interviews may be among the most rewarding exercises a marketing professional can master. It is, in fact, all about gaining wisdom through the art and science of asking the right person the right questions. Not only is it a productive exercise in focused inquiry—a type of critical thinking that is a valued professional skill—it is also the door to the essential insights that give marketing a competitive advantage.

With your list of contacts at hand, it's time to learn the basic principles that will allow you to engage buyers in interviews that will provide valuable information—information that buyers have never shared with your sales representatives or the competition.

Who Should Conduct the Interview?

Before we begin, let's take a moment to consider who in your organization is best suited to conduct the buyer interviews. And to make this easy, let's first talk about who should *not* conduct the interview. Answer: anyone who was ever involved in a sales call with this buyer.

If you are in marketing and are sometimes called in to assist with demonstrations, you are now disqualified from conducting an interview with those buyers. That's because we want buyers to be completely open with the interviewer about exactly what worked and what didn't as they went through their evaluation. Buyers' attitudes toward anyone who was a part of that assessment, whether positive or negative, will influence their reflection on the decision. Additionally, buyers are reluctant to share their whole story with anyone in a sales role, knowing full well that it is the salesperson's job to use these details to open up new conversations and sell something.

Apart from this prohibition on sales doing the interviews, anyone else would be a candidate. Ideally, we are looking for someone with an innate sense of curiosity. Someone who has an intrinsic interest in learning how things work, the dynamics that determine how decisions are made, the way parts in an organization fit together, and the manner in which options are weighed. We want someone who will keep an open mind to possibilities not known or considered, and not let personal knowledge and confidence act as a blinder. I've found trained journalists are among the best interviewers. They know how to inquire about things that they haven't been immersed in. They are quick studies and can unearth the important issues by asking relevant, unscripted follow-up questions.

Some companies will look for interviewers who are domain experts, including people who have previously been a customer of the organization. But this approach places even more pressure on the interviewer to keep an open mind.

In one remarkable example, an engineering corporation decided that their own product specialists should not conduct buyer interviews about the decisions for their own solutions. Instead the company asked their experts to trade places with their teammates, conducting interviews outside of their own field of expertise. They had noticed that those who knew less about the product had a greater ability to respond to their buyer's answers with probing questions, pursuing the buyer's story without the taint of preconceived opinions or knowledge.

Prepare for Your Buyer Interview

You'll want to do a little preparation prior to each interview so that you don't waste time during the call asking your buyer questions that can be answered in advance. Accurately note the buyer's name, role, and company using a reliable source. (It's always nice to casually inject the buyer's name into your questions during your talk, and having it written in front of you will remind you to do so.) A scan of the buyer's LinkedIn profile will give you some idea of the person's background and current position.

You'll want some basic information about the dates when the sale or evaluation took place, as this will help you appreciate how well the buyer will be able to remember and share the details of the story. Keep in mind that since we want to discover the specifics about the buyer's decision-making process—not about the specific product or service in particular—you need not be an expert on the product, but you should spend a few minutes on the company's website so you are generally familiar with the terminology the buyer is likely to use. You may also want to consult a product expert if there are aspects about features that you believe will arise in the conversation, such as specific perceived competitive advantages.

It helps to be familiar with facts about the evaluation and its outcome: whether a sale resulted, or if the buyer chose another option. (Should this information be unavailable, it shouldn't affect your questioning. Your interview will always start at the same place no matter the outcome.)

As an aid, have a legal pad handy and note in advance the pertinent information you may need to access during your conversation. It's odd how often we find ourselves unable to retrieve some facts when we are engaged in a detailed conversation and are feeling under a little stress. You'll also want to use that pad as a memory helper during the conversation. Even though we plan to record the conversation, you won't be able to take extensive notes.

Be sure to eliminate all distractions before doing the interviews. Turn off your cell phone, instant messaging, and email alerts. Your entire focus should be on the buyer. Active listening and responding with probing follow-up questions requires a lot of concentration, so distractions are a liability.

You'll also want to have access to a good method of recording the phone conversation. Being able to accurately capture the buyer's language is essential, and making a recording frees you from taking notes and allows you to concentrate on what the buyer is saying so that you can probe more deeply into their story. Don't even imagine you may be able to write down everything the buyer says; if you try, you risk falling behind and losing rapport with your interviewee.

As mentioned previously, it's advisable to have a colleague listen in on the interview. You'll find they can be of great help during a few minutes of reflecting about the conversation immediately after it has concluded. (Should you do so, be sure to introduce your colleague to the buyer at the beginning of the interview.)

Finally, before the conversation, you should return once again to the 5 Rings of Insight, and focus on your goal. You are going to try to understand what happened in the buyer's environment that triggered the search for a solution. You are also going to attempt to learn what steps were taken to investigate options, and discover what worked and what didn't work about that experience, and hear it expressed in the buyer's own words. We want to discern each step in the process and learn about every individual evaluation that resulted in a decision to continue to include our solution as an option, or exclude it from consideration.

Getting It on the Record

An audio recording of the phone call is incredibly valuable. But before you can push the "record" button, you need to obtain permission. It is unethical—as well as illegal in most states—not to obtain documented consent from the person being recorded. (An audio recording of the consent agreement is all the documentation necessary.) It is not advisable to ask for this permission when you first approach the buyer for the interview. If this request is introduced during the recruiting part of the project, some buyers get anxious and may think it necessary to get the approval of higher-level management or consult with company lawyers.

So plan to get the recording request out of the way at the beginning of the call. The best practice is to make this your first question prior to the actual interview, asking, "I really appreciate that you are able to take time to do this today. I'd like to capture everything you have to say, but I'm afraid that if I try to take notes I'll miss something. So before we get started, I would like permission to record this interview. The recording will not be shared with salespeople or anyone else except the small team working on this project with me. Would that be okay?"

Ninety-five percent of the time, the buyer will say, "Sure, that's fine," and the subject never comes up again. Four percent of the time the buyer will equivocate and say something like, "Well, yeah, I guess that's okay. But I won't be able to be as candid as you would like." In such a situation you need to make a decision: Should you cancel the recording, or make the recording and risk the possibility that this buyer will hold back and fail to share some great details with you? We've discovered after conducting hundreds of such interviews, the second option is the better choice. After a few minutes, the buyer will forget about the recording and the impact on the quality of the interview will be minimal. If you decide to abandon the recording, let's hope that you already invited a colleague to participate and they can take copious notes. (As noted earlier, you should not be attempting to take extensive notes while also conducting the interview.)

One percent of the time you will encounter someone who insists that you can't record it. In such a case, we recommend that you continue with the interview. You won't have the verbatim quotes to share in your Buying Insights, but you never want to pass up the opportunity to listen to what a buyer has to tell you.

"Take Me Back to the Day . . ."

Once the situation about making the recording is resolved, you are ready to dive in with your opening question. This is the only question that is scripted, as it is crucial for you and the buyer to focus immediately on the story of the evaluation and the decision-making process. It's tempting to try to defuse any possible nervousness with a bit of small talk that diverts the focus at the beginning of the conversation, but it's not productive. Asking, "Tim, how is your day going?" doesn't build rapport. In fact, this suggests that you aren't serious about the purpose of the call. (In our examples, we'll be using a fictional buyer named Tim, whom we are questioning about his evaluation of an automated email marketing system.)

So immediately after you've requested the recording, dive right in and say, "Tim, I know you're really busy. You're time's valuable, so I want to get right to our first question. Take me back to the day when you first decided to evaluate a new automated email marketing solution [or whatever category of solution your product fits into] and tell me what happened."

It's important to begin with a question about the moment when your buyer first became aware that a solution was needed—as opposed to when he first considered your product—because we are attempting to get him to focus on the moment when his organization first realized there was a problem that needed to be solved. This should have happened well before he ever encountered your product. This first question encourages the buyer to tell you about the triggering event that led to the search for a solution like yours. In our 5 Rings of Buying Insight, multiple responses to this question will lead you to understand the Priority Initiative insight.

Don't be surprised, however, if your buyer doesn't answer your stated question and responds instead with a short list of the benefits. For instance Tim might reply, "Well, we knew we needed to measure ROI for our marketing activities and we needed to get our campaigns to be more effective, so we decided to look into email marketing solutions." Frequently, this sentence is followed by a short story about how he found and selected a solution. In three minutes or less, you could conclude that Tim had told you the whole story. But he hasn't.

Remember that the Priority Initiative insight defines the triggering moment when the pain of living with the problem (or the positive associated with solving it) finally got this buyer persona's attention. We want to hear Tim talk about how this situation rose to the top of his to-do list, and what caused him to become willing to invest his time and budget on a solution like ours.

Use Your Buyer's Words to Probe for Insight

While your buyer is talking, you should be jotting notes on your legal pad. Just note a few keywords out of every sentence, so that you can return to some of these snippets with follow-up questions. When you do follow up, try to use the exact words that your buyer used to express his thoughts as you phrase your question.

The first probing question should be based on the benefits he mentioned at the beginning of his story. Think of this as a chance to help your buyer better understand (and answer) your question: "I want to go back to what you said about needing to measure marketing ROI, and to improve the effectiveness of your marketing campaigns. I'm sure that was a goal long before you started looking for this solution. What changed or occurred to make it a priority to start looking?"

At this point your buyer is likely to give you a much more detailed story about what was happening in his company, and he's likely to mention other senior-level buyer personas who played a decisive role. This is where you may learn that a new chief marketing officer (CMO) had expectations that could not be addressed, or that the chief executive officer's (CEO's) expansion plans included an entry into a new market, or that the chief financial officer (CFO) was responding to a regulatory change, to name just a few of the possible explanations. As your buyer tells this story, you should continue to jot a few words on your legal pad so that you can return later to probe into the expectations that each of these personas communicated to him. It's likely that these senior executives disappeared from the next few scenes in the story, so this is your opportunity to ask your buyer for details about any concerns or requirements that these other personas imposed on the decision.

Go Slowly to Capture the Whole Story

At any point in the buyer's narrative, he might jump forward chronologically in his story, skipping over the detailed insights that you need most. This often causes an inexperienced interviewer to begin probing at random moments in the narrative, which, in turn, makes gathering the entire story a lot more difficult.

Here's where your yellow legal pad is invaluable. While absorbing what the buyer is saying, jot down just a few key words—not many—about anything that captures your attention. Whenever your brain forms a thought like, "Gosh, I wish I could ask a question about this," rather than interrupt the buyer, just put an asterisk in the left column of the yellow pad. When you've thoroughly covered all of your questions about the earlier parts of your buyer's story, you can pick up the thread of what he already told you and ask a probing question that uses his exact words.

"You know, Tim, returning to what you just said a few minutes ago about [whatever may be a determining factor in the decision] . . . , what was important about that?"

Veteran TV talk show host Dick Cavett was particularly skilled at astutely directing the focus of the conversation back to an area that deserved greater scrutiny. He once observed, "If the person has strayed from an interesting topic, the direct approach usually works for getting them back. Just start that topic over again. Say, 'Let's go back to this,' or 'Let me steer you back to what you were more interesting about a minute ago.'"

Learning to interview is learning to listen actively, a skill that takes a lot more concentration than we might normally assume. Listening closely means not preparing the next question as the buyer is still answering your earlier inquiry. Even though the ability to multitask is a requirement stated in nearly every contemporary job description, it's not humanly possible to listen carefully, take verbatim notes about what is being said, and prepare the next question at the same time. Unskilled

interviewers often move on to the next question far too rapidly, leaving
follow-ups unasked, or they jump around in the chronology, asking
questions about the latter parts of their assessment rather than walking
the buyer slowly through every phase of their evaluation.

Questions That Keep the Conversation Flowing

In addition to listening actively, enabling the buyer to talk is
undoubtedly the other important interviewing skill to master.
Once the buyer has given his answer and stops talking, it's important
to be able to delve deeper into the story by asking a question that
builds on something the buyer has said.

We metaphorically refer to this as "pulling the thread," much as
you might slowly unravel a knitted sweater by tugging on a loose
strand. Let's look at another point in the interview and see how that
exchange might occur.

"Okay, Tim, so once you and the other executives decided that
this was the time to look for a new marketing automation solution,
what did you do to first evaluate your options?" Let's say that he
responded with, "Well, I started with an Internet search." This is not
an insight, but it is an opportunity to find out how much his Internet
search impacted his choice of vendors at this point in his story. Asking
the simple question, "How many vendors did you identify as a result
of that search?" anchors Tim at this point in his story, giving you a way
to define this stage in his evaluation. You can now ask the buyer about
this search experience with questions such as, "What information
were you hoping to find through this search?" and "Were there any
websites that were particularly helpful?" One of my favorite questions
is, "Were any of the companies you decided to consider unknown to
you prior to this search?" This inquiry helps to clarify whether this was
a perfunctory search or if, in fact, the Web research led your buyer to
evaluate a new option.

After you've explored the Internet search experience, you'll want to find out if there were other sources of information that were consulted to find potential solutions. Most of the time, there are at least three entirely different ways that buyers identify potential solutions, and if you fail to answer this question you will miss the critical insight that reveals how buyers find solutions like the one your organization offers.

During these first probing questions, a very interesting thing occurs. No one has ever before asked your buyer to talk at length about this experience, which may have involved weeks or months of painstaking research. By asking great follow-up questions in which you use many of the same words or phrases that the buyer voiced moments earlier, you're building a level of rapport that encourages him to engage with you at a deeper level. He now knows that you're not just robotically following a scripted series of questions for yet another marketing survey, but that you're actually listening to him and interested in the details of his story. Your questions are as simple as, "Tell me more about . . ." or "What was important about . . .," but they have prompted him to recall details that he has never spoken about previously, and he now knows that this is going to be a much more interesting conversation than he had expected.

As you walk the buyer through each part of his story, avoid thinking about the steps in the buying decision that you or your salespeople may have labeled with terms such as *research, evaluate, negotiate,* and so on. Buyers don't think this way, and these labels will interfere with your ability to uncover the whole story.

Similarly, you don't want to structure your interview around the 5 Rings of Buying Insight. This is a great format for presenting your interview findings so that they are useful to your marketing team, but it is a terrible way to get buyers to open up to you and tell you how they wrestle with the decision you want to influence. The questions in the 5 Rings don't work because they keep the focus on you and what you want to know. Your job is to keep the focus of the interview on the buyer and his story. Hone in on his narrative as he explains how he identified an urgent problem, researched the potential solutions, and gradually reduced the number of options until he found the one he considered to be a perfect fit. Don't worry; if he tells you his complete story and you ask the probing questions recommended in this chapter, you'll have all of the insights you need. We'll show you how to convert Tim's story into the 5 Rings of Buying Insight in the next chapter.

Once your buyer has talked about his search to find solutions worthy of evaluation, ask him how many possible solutions he decided to include. We aren't going to use that answer in the buyer persona, but his answer establishes a useful transition point in his story that you will use in your subsequent questioning. As the buyer is likely to remember selective details out of chronological order, you can reference this transition moment to return him to that point in his story.

An Example Interview with Tim

Let's look at part of an interview regarding Tim's search for an email marketing solution.

Interviewer: So once you guys decided you needed a new email marketing solution, what was the first action you took to figure out which possible solutions might meet these criteria?

Tim: Well, our marketing agency had already subscribed to a lot of different software platforms and turned to white papers and newsletters. So we were already aware of maybe a small subset; maybe two or three of these guys that we thought we could check into. We had a short punch list already based on those that we were aware of, and then just did a little more research on the Internet—looking at other competitors, looking at ratings websites. No, that's not the right term. Looking at industry sites that would rate the different tools and their pros and cons, checking out prices, requesting that the reps give us a call and answer questions, so a bunch of different little things.

Interviewer: Okay, so let's see . . . regarding the subset of agencies that you were already aware of, how many did you have top of mind, that you knew you wanted to look at? Was that a dozen, was it less than that?

Tim: It would have been like three . . . around three.

Interviewer: Okay, and when you went out on the Web, and you did a search, you must have come up with a lot more. How many did you come up with through your Web search that you didn't really know about before, but you thought, "These guys look interesting"?

Tim: Not as many as you'd think, because we really probably came up with only one or two more that we wanted to talk to beyond that. This is because we had a fairly specific kind of platform that we were looking for. There were some that were too small; in other words they didn't really have the features or capacity that we needed. And then there were a lot that were too big; they were more like our existing solutions which would still have required large setup fees and large ongoing fees. So it really came down to a pretty small set of only two or three.

Interviewer: This is interesting. Some were too small. And some too big and that would mean more setup costs. On the too small side, what would too small look like?

Tim: Well, there were some email marketing platforms that didn't really have the logic built in to do email marketing automation. Even though they might be easy to use and low cost, they didn't have the complexity of being able to set up behavioral rules to automate your marketing. So those were out. Or it wouldn't have the integrations we want with some of the CRMs our clients need.

It may appear that Tim and the interviewer were just having a nice chat, but during the conversation Tim revealed a number of great insights and quotes about the resources he trusted to alert him to quality solutions and his attitude as he did his Web research. And at the end of this exchange he elaborated on some of the specific expectations he had about solutions that were the right size for his needs.

Your ability to uncover insight is all about watching for wording in your buyer's answers that allow you to follow up. As you practice these interviews, you'll learn how easy it is to ask the buyer to expand on and tell you more about a comment that you jotted on your legal pad. Sometimes it can be as simple as, "That's interesting, Tim, what you said about the logic to do email marketing automation. Tell me more about that. . . ."

Look for Insight When Buyers Use Jargon

Another great probing opportunity arises whenever a buyer uses jargon to substitute for a more detailed descriptive explanation about some aspect of the decision or solution. You'll want to listen carefully. Some of these words are so familiar—*cutting-edge, flexible, market leading, industry-standard, scalable, world-class,* and *easy-to-use,* for example—you may let them pass by. However, not probing on them is a huge missed opportunity. This is your chance to uncover insight that explains precisely why this capability impresses your buyers. Undoubtedly, these same words and phrases appear in your competitors' marketing materials, but messaging that directly addresses the buyers' specific concerns cuts through the jargon and has the ability to catch their attention as if someone is speaking to them directly at the moment.

Refer to Figure 5.1 as a shortcut guide for probing whenever jargon occurs in the conversation.

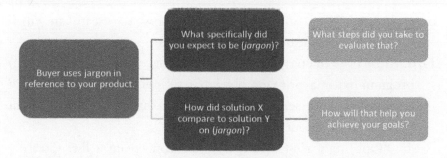

Figure 5.1 Example Probes on Jargon Reponses

Let's look at this example from our interview with Tim:

Interviewer: So, you just mentioned that you need a solution that is easy to use. Can you talk for a few minutes about what you evaluated around ease of use?

Tim: You know, just having a lot of templates and adding new templates. "Here are five new newsletter templates that are easy to use instantly." That's the first thing I would look for.

Interviewer: Okay.

Tim: The second thing I would look for is drag-and-drop capabilities. I want to add a new piece of content, if I want to add an image, if I want to add a video—it's just drag-and-drop. I want very little complication in terms of the backend work that you have to do to configure it.

Another thing is the, you know, having APIs [application programming interface] and hooks into other systems and social CRM systems that seamlessly integrate.

It's funny, when I was investigating how people use email systems, I finally realized that the primary way that they're used is around lists. Maybe it's common sense and maybe I should have figured that out, but, you know, lists are what drive the use of the system.

I have yet to find any of the email providers out there that say, "Here's how to use it. Here's the things you need to do, the steps you need to do that walk you through it." A how-to piece.

Interviewer: They walk you through how to create an email campaign, you mean?

Tim: More how to engage with your audience using email. "This is a program with a primary objective to generate awareness and demand for your services. Here are the three things you might want to think about doing.

"One, start a list. Well, how do you create a list? Create a landing page. What's on the landing page? The landing page talks about a newsletter. What does that newsletter do? It basically showcases the content," and on and on and on.

I don't know if you can hear it while reading this exchange, but I can still hear Tim's voice as he sensed my desire to hear him out. In the course of your probing, you'll need to determine just how much time you want to spend drilling down and gathering information on one topic. If you get someone like Tim on the phone, someone who is speaking at length about a particular aspect of the decision, keep probing and let him talk. On the other hand, if you find that the buyer isn't terribly engaged about a particular aspect of his story, it is best to move on. Remember that your job is to hear the buyer's story, and if their story doesn't include any time on your website, for example, don't dally there. Buyers will impart the most valuable insight while talking about their own experience, and you can get that information from a different interview with another buyer.

Make Your Questions about Your Impact Count

When the buyer mentions looking at a marketing resource that's important to you such as a website, white paper, or demo, you can learn a lot by asking, "How did the information you found there impact your choice of vendors?" Because you are in a conversation with the buyer who has already learned that you want a lot of detail, the buyer is likely to tell you what he or she remembers learning or experiencing as a result of the interaction. This is a far more important bit of information than just knowing that the buyer engaged with a particular type of marketing asset—this line of questioning can tell you which aspect of that asset made a decisive difference in the decision.

With high-consideration business-to-business (B2B) buying decisions it's likely that a key moment in the decision-making process happened when the buyer got to observe a demonstration of the product. Probing questions about the demo are an exceptionally useful way to learn about your buyer's impression of your competitors. Because this phase of the buying decision does not happen early in your buyer's story, you've likely spent enough time in conversation by this point to have built a rapport.

So be careful that you don't ruin the mood by asking for the names of the competitors or speculating about their identities. It is important to avoid questions that might provoke any discomfort, and remarkably, your buyer is likely to reveal far more detail if he or she hasn't shared any names. Once you have those details, it's likely that you can deduce the identities based on what you're told.

You will get some of the best insights at the transition points where buyers reduced the number of solutions they were evaluating, and the demo is one of the places where that usually occurs. This point in the narrative gives you a chance to ask buyers how they decided to exclude one of the options they found in the earlier part of the story, using a question such as: "You said you started with three solutions, but you mentioned only two came in for a demo. How did you decide to eliminate that third company from consideration?"

Please note carefully the wording of this last sentence, and that the first few words are "how did you decide." This is important phrasing for a couple of reasons. First, the alternative, "why did you decide," or any question that begins with a *why* can sound a bit confrontational. And second, "how did you decide" invites buyers to go deeper into that aspect of the story, revealing the actions they took, the information they evaluated, and the criteria that got your solution, or your competitor's, eliminated from consideration. This insight is pure gold.

Probing on Who Influences This Decision

Because most B2B decisions involve multiple buyer personas, you will want to discover as much information as possible about the others involved as your buyers tell the story about each stage of the buying decision. As they talk about researching solutions online or consulting their peers, for example, they may talk about the other people who were involved in that research. Or they may lead you to infer that they were doing all of the work by themselves. If they haven't directly addressed that point, it's a good idea to ask a probing question. "So you mentioned that 'we' were evaluating the input from the consultants. Who else was involved? I don't need names, just the roles of the other people."

Now you can begin to ask questions about how these other people factored into subsequent phases of the buyer's story. Through the buyer's eyes, you can identify the other buyer personas and begin to understand their impact on the outcome. You can ask the buyer to tell you whether any members of the selection team who witnessed the demo had voiced different opinions about the demos they saw, what they learned from that demo, and how that knowledge affected the decision to continue to evaluate the two solutions under consideration.

It's fascinating that in many instances you can actually learn more about the senior decision makers and their perceptions through your buyer's eyes than by interviewing them directly. This doesn't preclude the option to interview other buyers in the buying center, but it can give you most of the story if you don't have the opportunity to take that step.

Asking about the Perceived Value of Your Differentiators

Of the many types of probing questions in a buyer interview, there is one that requires concerted attention and care. This question has the potential to reveal significant insights, especially in instances where you know that the buyer did not choose your company's solution.

Figure 5.2 graphically illustrates a probing inquiry when the buyer has indicated that the solution that was not selected was too expensive. Your first question is "open-ended"—you are asking the buyer to recall anything that was available in the more expensive solution, but not in the one that was selected. With this question we find out whether or not the buyer can recall the characteristics that justify your premium pricing. This answer tells us whether our sales and marketing effort communicated the value but it wasn't important enough to justify the price, or if we simply failed to get the message across.

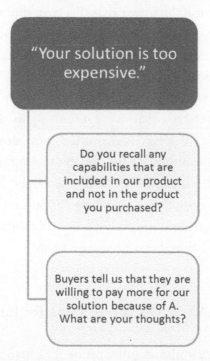

Figure 5.2   Example Probes on "It Was Too Expensive"

The next question, however, is even more interesting. In this follow-up question, you will want to have one or two statements that you have prepared in advance to test with buyers. You can change the statements for different interviews—especially if you find that buyers aren't reacting well to the first one you try—but the wording and the manner of framing this follow-up question is important. If it is stated slightly differently this question can sound as if it is actually a sales pitch, something that must be avoided. Here is the question: *"We are hearing from buyers that they are willing to pay more for our solution because it [the aspect of your product or service that is perceived to be a competitive advantage]. What are your thoughts on that?"*

With this question we have a rare chance to hear how the buyer views our perceived competitive advantage. If indeed the buyer was not aware of the advantage—a not uncommon situation—make sure not to transition into a sales pitch about your product's merits. Not only did you promise the buyer that this would not be a sales call, but your objective is to understand how buyers arrive at these conclusions.

Use this opportunity to record the buyer's knowledge about the perceived competitive advantage and whether it was viewed as important or disregarded during the evaluation. Because you are now aware of the steps that were involved in the buying process and what resources the buyer consulted, you now know where to concentrate your attention in the future: messaging that might need improvement; whether sales training should be refocused; and the language buyers respond to. Equally important, you'll be aware whether this competitive advantage is actually something your buyers value if and when they become aware of it.

When Features Affect Decisions, Look for Insight

In Figure 5.3 we examine a similar probe for situations where a specific feature missing from your solution appears to have been the decisive

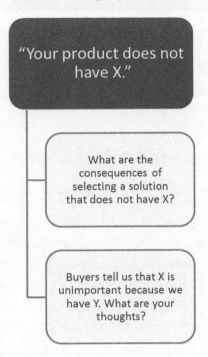

"Your product does not have X."

What are the consequences of selecting a solution that does not have X?

Buyers tell us that X is unimportant because we have Y. What are your thoughts?

**Figure 5.3   Example Probes on "Missing Feature"
Responses**

factor. (Once again, if you are interviewing a buyer about a product that you are not familiar with, talk with a product manager in advance to learn about any capabilities that might be alluded to in the course of this interview.) Initially, you want to find out what it is about this feature that buyers consider of importance. Second, you want to pose an open-ended question to gauge the magnitude of the buyer's concern about this feature by asking, "What consequences might result if you selected a solution that didn't have [the missing feature]?"

In the event the product manager informed you that this feature was not included because a workaround solution already existed, you want to ask a question that is worded similarly to the one we probed with when researching price as the decisive issue. You should ask, "We have heard from buyers that [the workaround solution] is important to them because they can do [the intended outcome when using the missing feature]. What are your thoughts about that?" Again the buyer's response will reveal a lot: You will find out if the buyer was aware of the workaround solution; whether it was evaluated; and if so, whether it was considered a viable approach or unacceptable.

First and Foremost, Be a Respectful Listener

Throughout the interview you always want to try to make it as easy as possible for your buyer to do the talking. Work on the flow of the conversation so that new questions logically follow up on given statements. Adding a little empathy early in the conversation can greatly ease what follows. For instance, suppose the buyer responds to your opening question about what triggered the search by saying, "We were under a lot of pressure to grow the number of leads we were generating for the sales pipeline." You can follow up with empathy and a probe by saying, "Yes, it seems like every marketer I know is concerned about leads. What do you think happened to make this initiative a priority at exactly that time?"

Silence can add a few awkward moments to any conversation, but sometimes it prompts someone to continue talking when a question hasn't been fully answered. By just saying, "Well, that's interesting. . . ." or by merely remaining silent you often cause the buyer to pick up the slack and give you additional detail.

This was another technique that Dick Cavett confessed yielded particularly revealing results. "You can hold someone with silence and make them go on," he said. "You tend to feel you need to fill all dead air. There are times when if you just say no more than 'uh-huh,' and pause, they'll add something out of a kind of desperation that turns out to be pretty good. Let them sweat a little and then they'll come up with something that they were perhaps not going to say."

Concentrate on the earliest stages of the buying process about which you have inadequate insight. When the buyer has covered a stage completely, you can easily transition to the next stage that followed by framing it as the next chapter in the story. Remember not to be concerned about staying on a script. By keeping brief notes on your legal pad and marking reminders whenever questions arise in your mind, you can resist the temptation to interrupt and know that you'll have the buyer's exact words to use when it's time to return to that part of the story.

As the buyer skips ahead in the story, you should feel comfortable slowing down the pace by saying, "Tim, I would like to return to what you said a few minutes ago about [the topic in question]. What you said was really interesting, but I wonder if you can tell me a little more about that." Be sure to refer to your brief notes and try to use phrases and expressions that the buyer voiced earlier.

Remember, never ask direct questions about you, your website, your campaigns, or your solutions. Make the conversation about the buyer's experience and you'll be rewarded with more information than you could ever obtain through direct questions.

Don't make the mistake of assuming you already know the answer to a question. One of the most common errors I note when observing people learning to conduct buyer interviews is a failure to probe on the buyer's statements. When I inquire why the interviewer failed to ask a follow-up, the most common answer is, "We hear that answer all the time; I already know what they'll say." Keep in mind that you need the buyer's words and verbatim quotes so that others on your team can hear your buyer speak this thought. Even if you've heard the answer a hundred times before, hearing this buyer's response in his or her own words still offers the possibility of a moment of clarity that transforms your understanding of the decision-making process. As Stephen Covey once wrote, "When you really listen to someone from their point of view, and reflect back to them that understanding, it's like giving them emotional oxygen."

Once you've gathered the information during the interview it's time for the next step—using it to build effective buyer personas.

6 | Mine Your Interviews for Buying Insights

It's a familiar scene from countless investigative police procedural dramas. The chief detective assembles the team and presents the evidence on a bulletin board. There are forensic photographs and images of witnesses and suspects. Pinned next to them is a detailed map of the crime scene, a timeline, photocopies of key evidence, and selected witness statements. This visual image is a powerful dramatic device that helps all observers understand the relevant personalities and clues (as well as red herrings) in the story.

Following your buyer interviews, you are going to engage in an exercise that has some parallels with the work of the chief detective. The stories we capture during our interviews will synthesize and prioritize the key elements of a narrative that has been a mystery until now.

But while the chief detective subjects the suspects' stories to a systematic analysis that gradually eliminates everyone except the prime suspect, we will do almost the reverse. We will combine all of the stories to create a single narrative that represents the mind-set of a group of buyers who think alike. When we are done, we will have a factual description of our person (or persons) of interest, and a story that details expectations, thinking, and decision-making process as that person approaches the decision you want to influence.

You Need Fewer Interviews Than You Expect

As you interview your first few buyers it's likely you will begin to hear very similar stories. You may get virtually identical answers to your questions about the buyers' Priority Initiatives, or people may have very similar concerns and barriers to choosing your solution.

However, before you begin to compile and aggregate your findings, it's a good rule to complete at least 8 to 10 buyer interviews. This doesn't mean that you won't complete additional interviews, but this is a good time to be aware of patterns and to compile your existing results.

While you are building your confidence in the interviewing methodology that we discussed in the last chapter, initiating this step after just a few interviews will help you to identify areas of the buyer's story where you haven't probed deeply enough. Don't worry about returning to the people you have already interviewed. Just make sure to focus on the missing areas in your upcoming interviews.

Once you are proficient with the interview techniques, you may be surprised to learn how few interviews it takes to discover all 5 Rings of Buying Insight. Your decision about how many interviews to conduct will be easier if you think about buyer persona insight as a tool to cut through the clutter and tell you exactly what you need to do. Now you can see that marketing based on intuition and guesswork is a blunt axe, and that insights culled from a small group of interviews is akin to a Swiss Army knife. This degree of acuity is relatively easy to achieve and much sharper than anything you've ever had in your toolkit. For most marketing decisions and objectives, this is perfectly aligned with the job at hand.

However, there are times when the goal is so critical, or the need to convince other decision makers so compelling, that you will need even more precision. In this relatively rare situation you want a tool that is as sharp as a surgeon's scalpel.

This is the time to validate your interview findings with a survey across a large population of buyers. A professional research firm can help you build this survey around the insights derived from your buyer interviews. The research firm will help you to choose the number of participants in the survey, and they will know how to ask questions in multiple ways to eliminate opportunities for error. This exercise rapidly yields statistically valid data that is more convincing and far more efficient than, for example, doubling the number of buyer interviews you conduct before building your buyer personas.

Should you be a marketer working in-house, we recommend that you continue to conduct buyer interviews on a regular basis, attempting to complete one each month. You are unlikely to gain significant new insights from these interviews in the near term, but when change does occur you will be the first to know. In addition you will have the credibility at internal meetings to say, "I just spoke to a buyer last week, and she said. . . ."

Like the chief detective, we need to categorize and prioritize our research into a succinct, easily understood format so that we can be sure we didn't miss anything. We have limited resources available to locate and capture our suspects, so we must convert reams of interview data into a concise and revealing story that motivates the team, aligning everyone to execute the most productive strategy.

Step 1: Mark Up Your Interview Transcript

As soon as you complete an interview, send your recorded interview to a transcription service to have it converted into a written document. A simple Web search will lead you to dozens of companies that accept online file uploads. Any of them can usually complete the transcription in less than a week for a charge of roughly $1 per minute.

Don't skip this step, as your interview transcripts contain the verbatim quotations that will make your buyer personas speak from the heart, voicing the real concerns and attitudes that your stakeholders need to hear.

With the first transcript open on your computer, read the interview from the beginning. When you find a quotation that answers one of the questions in the 5 Rings of Buying Insight, use the comments feature in your word processing software to highlight the quotation and label it with the relevant insight.

Because you started the interview by asking buyers about their Priority Initiative, you are likely to find quotations early on that help you to convey the triggering events and people that set the decision-making process in motion. Mark any quotations that answer this question with a "PI" for Priority Initiatives.

As you continue to read your buyer's story, you will find quotations about the changes buyers expected to gain from this solution—these should be marked "SF" for Success Factor. Remember that Success Factors sound like benefits statements, so keep an eye out specific business or practical outcomes as well as personal aspirational statements.

You will find Perceived Barriers "PB" insights throughout the interview, and especially in the places where you probed about how the buyer eliminated a few solutions from consideration. Buyers will also speak early in their stories about the barriers that prevented them from addressing this problem much sooner. Perceived Barriers often focus on people who got in the way, previous negative experiences, or capabilities that are missing from some solutions.

The questions that probed on how buyers eliminated options or why they kept certain solutions under consideration will also give you quotations that you can mark as Decision Criteria "DC." These differ from the other insights because they describe the specific features or

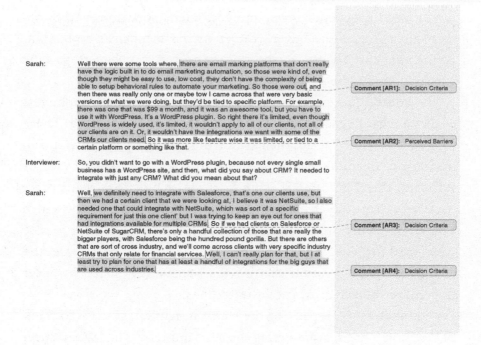

Figure 6.1   Example Interview Transcript Mark-Up

capabilities of the company or solution that were most important to your buyer. You will also find these quotations in response to your probing questions about what the buyer wanted to learn while reading a white paper, visiting a website, or attending a demo.

As you read through your buyer's story, mark quotations "BJ" for the Buyer's Journey insight whenever it describes who was involved in the decision and what the buyer did to evaluate options.

Not all the insights you mark on the transcript will fall easily within these five neat categories; some comments may encompass two insight categories simultaneously. In particular, the differences between Success Factors and Decision Criteria seem to cause confusion.

As a shorthand aid, think of Success Factors as benefits: scenarios that buyers believe will change after they complete this purchase. These might range from results that directly relate to the company's Priority Initiative—for instance, growing revenue by enabling a more personalized experience for online customer transactions—to things that might impact the buyer's career or the company's reputation. Remember that Success Factors communicate your buyers' specific expectations for the *outcomes* that matter most to them.

By contrast, Decision Criteria are the *capabilities* that your buyers evaluate regarding each of the solutions they are considering. These insights tell you what tips the balance in favor of a particular option during the decision-making process. In the case of hardware or software, these are often specific features or functions that matter decisively to the buyer. Buyers might also emphasize the importance of a service function, for instance, "We want to work with people who treat us like we're important." Decision Criteria are the attributes of the solution that buyers believe they need in order to achieve their Success Factor outcomes.

Another way of separating these two insight categories is to think of Decision Criteria as answering the *what* and *how* (as in "What aspect of the solution is critically decisive, and how does it do this?"), while Success Factors answer the *why* ("Why is this aspect important to the organization?").

There are situations in which a buyer's Success Factors and Decision Criteria are linked. For a fictional example, imagine a software feature called CyberReaderPlus, a real-time interface that allows Web visitors to interact with a virtual associate, much like they would at a public library information desk. In this example, CyberReaderPlus is a standard feature provided by most companies in this market.

A small entrepreneur you interviewed about his search for a Web software solution told you: "We wanted a software solution that works like CyberReaderPlus because it will give us the appearance of a far bigger, more sophisticated and established firm, without breaking the bank. It will allow us to have real-time access to customer conversations and be alerted on a dashboard if any conversations vary from the norm." We would capture the first sentence in this quotation as a Success Factor because it tells us *why* this feature is important. But the second sentence would be captured under Decision Criteria because it answers the *what* question: "It will allow us to have real-time access to customer conversations and be alerted on a dashboard if any conversations vary from the norm." Although both of these insights directly refer to the CyberReaderPlus feature, the Success Factor insight explains the reason *why,* while the Decision Criteria answers the *what.*

As you scrutinize more buyer interviews and contemplate how the insights revealed during the course of the conversations define the buyer's mind-set, you will become better attuned to distinguishing the important yet subtle differences between these two crucial insight categories.

Step 2: Organize the Story Based on Buying Insights

You now need to choose which of the many quotations that you have highlighted will best communicate the insights you captured during the interviews. You will likely have dozens of quotations highlighted in each interview, but you can't expect your stakeholders to read all of them. Instead you need to choose the most insightful quotations, those where the buyer disclosed the details and emotions that had the greatest impact on the choice of solutions.

The easiest way to do this is to use a spreadsheet program such as Excel to build an "Insights Aggregator" that is made up of five tabulated worksheets, naming one for each of the 5 Rings of Buying Insight. See Figure 6.2.

On each worksheet, label column A for the buyer quotes. The second, column B, is where you will note the interview that was the source of the quotation. Column C is used to create a shorthand summary of the key points contained in the insight quotation. And finally, we'll use column D to reflect on possible segmentation options. For the first part of this process, we'll fill in only columns

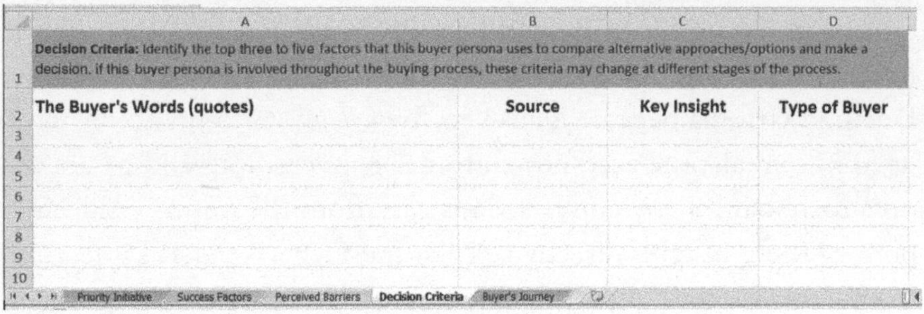

Figure 6.2   Insights Aggregator Spreadsheet

A and B. After we have all of the quotations from all of the interviews pasted into those two columns, we'll return to columns C and D, where we will begin to analyze the quotations we've collected.

Once you have the worksheet built, start with your first marked up interview and begin to paste quotations into column A of the Insights Aggregator. As you insert the quotation into the worksheet, don't forget to identify the source of the interview (in column B) where this quotation originated, as you will need that detail in the steps that follow.

You should be able to move quickly through each interview, copying quotations in whatever order they appear in the interview and clicking around on the tabs, pasting quotations into the correct worksheet. As you move through this step, you may notice that you marked up quotations that are not as useful as those you marked in other parts of the interview. Feel free to skip any quotations that are not compelling or, if you prefer, paste them all into the worksheet and attend to the culling of less useful quotations once they are all in one place.

You'll note that our illustration of the tabbed worksheet includes a summary definition of each of the 5 Rings of Buying Insight at the top of each page. As you cut and paste your buyer's quotations into this worksheet, this will help you remember the question your buyer's quotation is meant to answer. When you complete this step, your worksheet will look like the one in Figure 6.3.

A	B	C	D
Decision Criteria: Identify the top three to five factors that this buyer persona uses to compare alternative approaches/options and make a decision. If this buyer persona is involved throughout the Buying Process, these criteria may change at different stages of the process.			
The Buyer's Words (quotes)	**Source**	**Key Insight**	**Type of Buyer**
There are email marketing platforms that don't really have the logic built in to do email marketing automation, so even though they might be easy to use and low cost, they don't have the complexity of being able to set up behavioral rules to automate your marketing. So those are out.	Sarah, agency marketer		
There was one that was $99 a month, and it was an awesome tool, but you have to use it with WordPress. It's a WordPress plug-in. So it's limited. It wouldn't apply to all of our clients. Not all of our clients are on it. Or it wouldn't have the integrations we want with some of the customer relationship management (CRM) systems our clients need.	Sarah, agency marketer		
A large enterprise, you know, maybe the process changes in terms of proper branding guidelines, et cetera, et cetera, but just having a lot of templates and adding new templates, here's five new newsletter templates that are easy to use instantly. That's the first thing I would look for.	Chris, in-house marketer	\	
That I can have multiple lists on multiple topics, all funneling into a single account with separate forms, confirmations, autoresponders, the whole bit, for each channel.	Chris, in-house marketer		
They had templates, but they also had templates that were integrated into the plug-ins. One could just create the newsletter within their plug-in and just format it quite easily, and add a photograph. That was quite a big thing because it meant that at some point they wouldn't need to rely on me to do it for them.	Frank, agency marketer		
We have a fairly specific kind of platform that we are looking for, and there are some that are too small, without the features or capacity we need. Then there are a lot that are too big, more like our existing solutions that require large setup and ongoing fees. So it really comes down to only two or three options.	Frank, agency marketer		

Figure 6.3 Insights Aggregator—Cut and Paste Quotations

Step 3: Write a Headline for Each Key Insight

Once you have pasted the quotations into the relevant parts of the Insights Aggregator, it is time to write a short statement or "headline" for each of the quotations. Starting with the Priority Initiative tab, read each quotation and write a few words in column C—the "Key Insight" column of the Insights Aggregator—that communicates the key point explaining what triggered the buyer's search for a solution. As you continue to read the quotations you have selected, you should adjust the wording of your Key Insight headline so that similar quotations can be listed together with the same inclusive Key Insight headline. Once you have completed this step on your Priority Initiative worksheet, you can use the sort feature in your spreadsheet program to group related quotations together. Repeat this for each of the other four insights and your worksheet will look like Figure 6.4.

Now it's time to select the Buyer Quotes and Key Buying Insights that you will use in your buyer persona. Once your worksheet is sorted by the Key Insight, a quick scan will tell you how many quotations you have for each of the headlines you created in column C.

First have a look at the Key Buying Insights where you have several quotations, checking to see if they each came from different buyer interviews, as will be indicated in column B. If two or more of the quotations are from the same buyer interview, delete the one that is least useful and retain the one that conveys the most compelling detail about that buyer's expectations. You don't want to use multiple quotations from one buyer interview to support any Key Insight.

Next look to see if you still have any Key Buying Insights that have four or more quotations from different buyers. If these are all compelling quotations, think about whether you could write even more detailed, compelling headlines by assigning two of the quotations to a newly written Key Insight. See Figure 6.5 (before you adjust the Key Insight) and Figure 6.6 (after you adjust the Key Insight label). As you will notice, the Key Insight headlines are now far more specific

A	B	C	D
Decision Criteria: Identify the top three to five factors that this buyer persona uses to compare alternative approaches/options and make a decision. If this buyer persona is involved throughout the Buying Process, these criteria may change at different stages of the process.			
The Buyer's Words (quotes)	**Source**	**Key Insight**	**Type of Buyer**
It seemed WYSIJA was the appropriate choice. First because they charged more—they charged $99 per year. We felt that they would be able to provide more support because they were being paid more, if we did need the support. They also had an option to use their own servers, because what we were doing was that it was being transmitted through our own server.	Frank, agency marketer	Ability to send from our own or others' servers	
There are email marketing platforms that don't really have the logic built in to do email marketing automation, so even though they might be easy to use and low cost, they don't have the complexity of being able to set up behavioral rules to automate your marketing. So those are out.	Sarah, agency marketer	Combination of easy setup and automated marketing	
One of the things that was important to us was that we wanted a really easy solution and we also wanted the autoresponder.	Wayne, in-house marketer	Combination of easy setup and automated marketing	
A large enterprise, you know, maybe the process changes in terms of proper branding guidelines, et cetera, et cetera, but just having a lot of templates and adding new templates, here's five new newsletter templates that are easy to use instantly. That's the first thing I would look for.	Chris, in-house marketer	Ease of use	
They had templates, but they also had templates that were integrated into the plug-ins. One could just create the newsletter within their plug-in and just format it quite easily, and add a photograph. That was quite a big thing, because it meant that at some point they wouldn't need to rely on me to do it for them.	Frank, agency marketer	Ease of use	
I don't want to spend money having someone build us templates. I want to be able to repurpose something that's already there. Make it look like ours, but I want to take something that's there that I really like and be able to be able to easily customize it, if you will.	Wayne, in-house marketer	Ease of use	

Figure 6.4 Insights Aggregator—Write Key Insight Headlines

A	B	C	D

Decision Criteria: Identify the top three to five factors that this buyer persona uses to compare alternative approaches/options and make a decision. If this buyer persona is involved throughout the Buying Process, these criteria may change at different stages of the process.

The Buyer's Words (quotes)	Source	Key Insight	Type of Buyer
A large enterprise, you know, maybe the process changes in terms of proper branding guidelines, et cetera, et cetera, but just having a lot of templates and adding new templates, here's five new newsletter templates that are easy to use instantly. That's the first thing I would look for.	Chris, in-house marketer	Easy to use	
They had templates, but they also had templates that were integrated into the plug-ins. One could just create the newsletter within their plug-in and just format it quite easily, and add a photograph. That was quite a big thing, because it meant that at some point they wouldn't need to rely on me to do it for them.	Frank, agency marketer	Easy to use	
Of course it's easy to use. Everyone's saying theirs is easy to use. So it is a major criteria for me to see which one allows me to get to my goal before I have to consult help or call anybody. If it's easy to use, then I should be able to figure it out.	Pam, in-house marketer	Easy to use	
Very little complication in terms of the backend work that you have to do to configure it. Another thing is the, you know, having application program interface (APIs) and hooks into other systems such as Nimble and other social CRM systems that seamlessly integrate easily, and it can be done.	Paul, in-house marketer	Easy to use	
I don't want to spend money having someone build us templates. I want to be able to repurpose something that's already there. Make it look like ours, but I want to take something that's there that I really like and be able to easily customize it, if you will.	Wayne, in-house marketer	Easy to use	
When I want to add a new piece of content, add an image or a video, I want to simply drag-and-drop.	Wendy, agency marketer	Easy to use	

Figure 6.5 Insights Aggregator—Before Adjusting Key Insights

Decision Criteria: Identify the top three to five factors that this buyer persona uses to compare alternative approaches/options and make a decision. If this buyer persona is involved throughout the Buying Process, these criteria may change at different stages of the process.

A	B	C	D
The Buyer's Words (quotes)	**Source**	**Key Insight**	**Type of Buyer**
A large enterprise, you know, maybe the process changes in terms of proper branding guidelines, et cetera, et cetera, but just having a lot of templates and adding new templates, here's five new newsletter templates that are easy to use instantly. That's the first thing I would look for.	Chris, in-house marketer	A lot of high quality, easy to update templates	
They had templates, but they also had templates that were integrated into the plug-ins. One could just create the newsletter within their plug-in and just format it quite easily, and add a photograph. That was quite a big thing, because it meant that at some point they wouldn't need to rely on me to do it for them.	Frank, agency marketer	A lot of high-quality, easy-to-update templates	
I don't want to spend money having someone build us templates. I want to be able to repurpose something that's already there. Make it look like ours, but I want to take something that's there that I really like and be able to easily customize it, if you will.	Wayne, in-house marketer	A lot of high-quality, easy-to-update templates	
Of course it's easy to use. Everyone's saying theirs is easy to use. So it is a major criterion for me to see which one allows me to get to my goal before I have to consult help or call anybody. If it's easy to use, then I should be able to figure it out.	Pam, agency marketer	I should be able to figure it out on my own	
Very little complication in terms of the backend work that you have to do to configure it. Another thing is the, you know, having APIs and hooks into other systems such as Nimble and other social CRM systems that seamlessly integrate easily, and it can be done.	Paul, in-house marketer	I should be able to figure it out on my own	
When I want to add a new piece of content, add an image or a video, I want to simply drag-and-drop.	Wendy, agency marketer	I should be able to figure it out on my own	

Figure 6.6 Insights Aggregator—After Adjusting Key Insights

and valuable for your marketing team, providing even more useful details about your buyer's expectations.

Conversely, for Key Buying Insights that have only one quotation, consider consolidating these under a Key Insight headline that expresses what two or more of these quotations have in common. But don't force a connection if one doesn't exist. For quotations that are truly outliers, leave them on the spreadsheet until additional data supports their inclusion in your buyer persona.

If you plan to follow up your interviews and validate your findings with a survey, give all of the results of this step, including those from only one interview, to your research firm. You will want to test each of the Key Buying Insights on your spreadsheet regardless of how many people gave you that information.

When you have completed the interviews and organized your findings based on the 5 Rings of Buying Insight, you have a very clear picture of the factors that drive your buyers' decisions. You have probably mined more than 100 pages of transcribed interviews to find the quotations that best depict your buyers' mind-set as they wrestled with the decision you want to influence. Through these quotations, you will be able to reveal the essence of your buyer's story in a relatively brief narrative that will guide your team's most critical marketing decisions.

Before we talk about how you can use your buyer personas, we want to show you how you can use these insights to determine how many buyer personas you need. This is such an important issue that we decided to give this crucial topic a chapter of its own.

7 | Determine How Many Buyer Personas You Need

It is likely that one of your first thoughts about buyer personas included an estimate of how many you need to build. In fact, we wouldn't be surprised if you skipped right to this section. So first the good news: You need far fewer buyer personas than you may think. The bad news: You'll need to interview your buyers and follow the guidance in these next few pages to determine the answer.

There is a lot of tension around this question and for good reason. As you begin to build buyer personas that represent real people, you will inevitably be tempted to "humanize" your persona with a wide array of interesting details. This often begins when you decide to include the fact that your chief executive officer (CEO) buyer persona is male, married, and extroverted. Although this might not seem like a problem at first, eventually someone will note that many CEOs are female, single, and introverted. Someone else will point to the female CEOs who are married with children.

The apparently harmless decision to add attributes to your buyer persona can thus spark debate about its credibility. Worse yet, because each of the attributes you include could potentially be used to differentiate one group of buyers from another, you may feel compelled to create another persona.

Things were so much easier when marketers didn't need to tell a different version of their story to different types of buyers. Before the Internet made information so easy to access, buyers had no choice but to pick up the phone early in their buying decision. Sales had the perfect opportunity to build segments of one—understanding a single buyer's needs and presenting their company's solution as a perfect fit.

Now that buyers eliminate all but one or two sellers from consideration before they talk to a salesperson, marketing must achieve a more difficult task—understanding the needs of groups of buyers and establishing that same perfect fit.

Thus, the fundamental question isn't how many buyer personas are required, but rather how many ways do you need to market your solution so that you can persuade buyers that your approach is ideally suited to their needs. We can achieve this goal only if the way we define our buyer personas makes it easy to know when a different version of our story will result in more business for the company.

Segment Buyers Based on Insights, Not Profiles

Think about someone you know well, a close friend or relative, and I'm sure you could readily relate descriptive facts such as age, marital status, ethnicity, number of children, hobbies, education, profession, and geographic location. The specificity of this type of data would make it easy to group your friend with other people who are in the same demographic categories and identify the traits that distinguish him or her from other people.

As we discussed in Chapter One, some marketers think that personas should include their "psychographic" profile, as this allows us to group buyers based on characteristics such as personality traits, opinions, aspirations, and concerns. Thinking again about your friend, we're sure that you could add a wide range of descriptors in these categories.

Business-to-business (B2B) marketers often exercise a variation on the demographic approach to grouping buyers when they begin with an existing segmentation model—revolving around company size, geographic location, and/or industry—and include an added dimension based on the role of the buying influencer. You can see how an industry-oriented company that focuses on five industries might now conclude that it needs three buyer personas to represent the role of each influencer in each industry. This company would conclude that three buyers in five industries translate into 15 buyer personas, or even more if they begin to include the personal demographics or psychographics you used to describe your friend.

This is just one example. You will likely struggle with too many buyer personas if you believe that any aspect of your Buyer's Profile—demographics, psychographics, or combinations of both—should define how many personas you may need. Fortunately, there is a far more efficient option. Instead of grouping buyers based on who they are, you can group them based on your Buying Insights, which reveal the differences in their expectations about doing business with you.

Imagine that you want to help a real estate agent prepare to show apartments to the friend described earlier. The agent might be able to intuit some of your friend's apartment preferences if you provided a lengthy profile of your friend, replete with all of the demographic and psychographic data we discussed. Or you could simply tell the real estate agent about your friend's desire for proximity to mass transit service, local restaurants, and running trails.

In this story it is easy to see that a salesperson derives far more value from your Buying Insights than they would from your most comprehensive Persona Profile. The realtor's ability to create a compelling match between your friend's needs and the "product" is much easier to achieve when the salesperson understands the buyer's expectations for this decision.

This single version of a buyer's story matches our own experience with the multiple stories that we discover and communicate through Buying Insights. When we group people together who are like-minded with respect to their expectations when doing business with us, we get the most actionable guidance about how we can match our solution to their needs.

Because marketers of low-consideration solutions cannot interview their buyers to discover Buying Insights, their buyer personas will generally revolve around the demographic and psychographic details in Buyer Profiles.

But marketers of medium- to high-consideration solutions, those of us who have the privilege of listening to our buyers' stories about the decisions we want to influence, can define our buyer personas based on what buyers tell us directly about the factors that impact their decisions. We can determine the optimal number of buyer personas and, more critically, the need for differentiated marketing efforts by analyzing what we learned about the 5 Rings of Buying Insight.

Conduct More Interviews to Test Segmentation Options

Many companies initiate their buyer persona research because they want to know how to differentiate their marketing strategies for different types of buyers. This is often driven by a desire to market to buyers who had previously been uninvolved in the decision-making process, but who are now either influencing or complicating deals and resulting sales. In other instances a company has a business strategy that involves expansion into new market segments. In B2B transactions, a company may be uncomfortable with the realization that they haven't been marketing to everyone involved in a complex sale.

Marketers who have the resources to support differentiated marketing strategies may decide to test their hypothesis by interviewing people believed to represent different points of view. The decision to conduct additional interviews, however, will obviously entail additional work and investment. Should an outside research firm undertake the research, this will increase the cost of the buyer personas. So before engaging in this option, it's wise to consider this carefully.

We suggest that you begin any assessment such as this by assembling your stakeholders and reviewing each of the 5 Rings of Buying Insight. During the discussion, determine whether the group believes the insights are likely to vary enough to justify any additional investment. Sometimes a company will decide that it is far more efficient to conduct interviews with one segment only, followed by a survey of a statistically valid sample to determine whether the findings apply to the other segments as well.

For example, a global manufacturer of engineering components wanted to understand an engineering buyer who is essential to their marketing success. When they first approached us they expected to conduct research in each of four regions: Latin America, North America, Europe, and Asia. We held a meeting to discuss the 5 Insights, beginning with the Priority Initiative.

We suspected that the factors that would trigger the engineer's search for a new supplier of these components would not vary across geographic regions. Over the course of a 1-hour meeting, we went on to discuss the buyer's likely Success Factors, Perceived Barriers, Decision Criteria, and Buyer's Journey. By the end of the meeting we had decided that the Buying Insights would likely be very similar across all geographies, with the exception of the Buyer's Journey.

The company agreed that the best approach was to conduct all of the interviews in North America. To verify these results, we agreed to a second step, a survey that would test all of the Buying Insights in each of these geographic regions.

In other instances we've seen this discussion lead to a decision to conduct interviews in each segment. One client decided it was necessary to segment interviews based on the size of the target company, because the company's salespeople were experiencing more difficulty closing deals in the midmarket category and wanted to see how the buying decisions differed compared with the enterprise category.

Other marketers want to understand how senior executives view the buying decision—a buyer that salespeople often refer to as the "decision maker." This label describes only one aspect of the buying decision, however, as our interviews reveal that the senior executive rarely influences the choice of suppliers. In a high-consideration decision, a senior executive frequently triggers the search for a new solution, setting the agenda for the decisions that others will make as they evaluate alternative approaches and eliminate all options, save one or two. Once a team of internal stakeholders has completed their assessment, this senior executive generally hears the team's recommendation and approves the choice the others have made.

Some marketers choose to interview the senior executives to learn more about the details that trigger the investment, even though this buyer can tell them far less about the expectations that factor into the company's choice of solutions. Others will rely on the midlevel buyer to reveal the boss's agenda so that they can learn exactly which marketing activities have the greatest impact on the selection. A few will decide to interview both stakeholders.

Three factors ultimately determine whether a company should choose to interview additional buyers to discover different perspectives. Firstly, does your company have the capacity to market to the differentiated groups of buyers that this research may reveal? Secondly, is your company able to invest time or money to conduct additional interviews? And, finally, you will want to engage in a bit of educated guesswork about how many different insights the additional interviews are likely to reveal.

The decision to interview different types of buyers is a judgment call requiring careful consideration. It's unnecessary to interview every role in the buying center just because there are many different participants, or to automatically decide that you must conduct interviews in every region, geography, or industry where you do business.

Analyze Insights to Decide How Many Personas

In the last chapter you learned how to mine your interviews for insightful buyer quotations, weigh the meaning in each one, group them based on similar thoughts, and write headlines that communicate the Key Buying Insights. These are the first steps to determine how many ways you need to group buyers so that you can persuade them to choose you.

If every buyer you interviewed related very similar Buying Insights, you will need only one buyer persona to guide the decisions we will discuss in the upcoming chapters. However, if you find that some of the buyers you interviewed had different expectations than others, you will want to take one more step to decide whether two buyer personas will help you create a more persuasive marketing strategy.

In the simplest example, the differences you discovered will be aligned with a readily apparent demographic attribute. For example, as a marketer for a manufacturer of construction equipment you conduct buyer interviews with equipment rental companies. Your Buying Insights research reveals distinctive differences in the Decision Criteria and Success Factors for firms renting to two contrasting types of customers: professional contractors and do-it-yourself homeowners. The first group of companies renting to professionals may prefer advanced features even if the equipment requires considerable skill and experience to operate, while the second group might be willing to sacrifice features in favor of equipment that anyone can use. Because your manufacturing company has a great answer for both types of buyer expectations, you decide that having two buyer personas would guide your marketing team to tell a differentiated and compelling story to each of these distinct audiences.

Another example of a demographic approach to segmentation is depicted in Figure 7.1. Here we see the Insights Aggregator spreadsheet that we created in the last chapter, with a new column headed "Type of Buyer." In this column, you can see that the researcher is assessing whether the trigger to buy an email marketing solution is the same for in-house and agency marketers.

For in-house marketers, the trigger was their organization's decision to put more emphasis on digital marketing. The buyers who worked in marketing agencies had a different perspective. Although their core business had long included digital marketing, the agency marketer's need for a solution was linked to an expansion into new market segments.

Figure 7.2 shows another tab from this study, the Decision Criteria insight. Here we see that both agency and in-house marketers share the need for solutions that work much like other software they currently use with regularity, as well as deliver lots of easily customizable templates and allow for behavioral rules that automate marketing.

We have now found two insight categories where there are differences between these buyers' expectations. Does this email marketing solution provider need two buyer personas or only one?

Will Two Buyer Personas Help You Win More Business?

To answer this question, you will want to consider the extent to which the differences you discovered are relevant to your ability to

A	B	C	D
Priority Initiative: What changes trigger this buyer persona's search for this solution? What about this buyer persona's circumstances cause this problem to be funded for resolution?			
The Buyer's Words (quotes)	**Source**	**Key Insight**	**Type of Buyer**
The CEO decided that we needed to get serious in the digital space. He hired a new vice president (VP) of digital strategy and innovation, who came up with a vision for how to make it work for the seven companies we owned.	Jason, in-house marketer	A new investment in digital communications	In-house marketer
As a content producer and curator, I thought it would make sense that once a month, and only once a month, I would create a newsletter that would have only "the best of the best", and send it to my followers, customers, and prospective customers.	Chris, in-house marketer	A new investment in digital communications	In-house marketer
Our sales were starting to flatten out a little bit, so we were talking about different ways that we could help our sales force do better follow-ups. And one of the options was email marketing.	Wayne, in-house marketer	A new investment in digital communications	In-house marketer
We were looking for a solution that would be a better fit for the leads we were starting to see from small- to medium-sized businesses. These smaller companies were going to be good clients for us, but they weren't going to have the budget for the setup costs that our existing solution required. High upfront costs would be such a barrier that we might not win their business.	Sarah, agency marketer	Meet the needs of specific segments of clients	Agency marketer
Our client was doing email through an agency, a copywriter who sent the emails for them. But my client didn't have any insight into the data or statistics. I said look, you should really be far more on top of this and let's look for an appropriate system for you guys.	Irene, agency marketer	Meet the needs of specific segments of clients	Agency marketer

Figure 7.1   Analyze Priority Initiative by Type of Buyer

119

Decision Criteria: Identify the top three to five factors that this buyer persona uses to compare alternative approaches/options and make a decision. If this buyer persona is involved throughout the Buying Process, these criteria may change at different stages of the process.

A	B	C	D
The Buyer's Words (quotes)	**Source**	**Key Insight**	**Type of Buyer**
A large enterprise, you know, maybe the process changes in terms of proper branding guidelines, et cetera, et cetera, but just having a lot of templates and adding new templates, here's five new newsletter templates that are easy to use instantly. That's the first thing I would look for.	Chris, in-house marketer	A lot of high-quality, easy-to-update templates	In-house marketer
They had templates, but they also had templates that were integrated into the plug-ins. One could just create the newsletter within their plug-in and just format it quite easily, and add a photograph. That was quite a big thing, because it meant that at some point they wouldn't need to rely on me to do it for them.	Frank, agency marketer	A lot of high-quality, easy-to-update templates	Agency marketer
I don't want to spend money having someone build us templates. I want to be able to repurpose something that's already there. Make it look like ours, but I want to take something that's there that I really like and be able to easily customize it, if you will.	Wayne, in-house marketer	A lot of high-quality, easy-to-update templates	In-house marketer
Of course it's easy to use. Everyone's saying theirs is easy to use. So it is a major criteria for me to see which one allows me to get to my goal before I have to consult help or call anybody. If it's easy to use, then I should be able to figure it out.	Pam, agency marketer	I should be able to figure it out on my own	Agency marketer
Very little complication in terms of the backend work that you have to do to configure it. Another thing is the, you know, having APIs [application programming interfaces] and hooks into other systems such as Nimble and other social CRM [customer relationship management] systems that seamlessly integrate easily, and it can be done.	Paul, in-house marketer	I should be able to figure it out on my own	In-house marketer
When I want to add a new piece of content, add an image or a video, I want to simply drag-and-drop.	Wendy, agency marketer	I should be able to figure it out on my own	Agency marketer

Figure 7.2 Analyze Decision Criteria by Type of Buyer

5 Rings of Buying Insight	Agency Marketer	In-House Marketer
Priority Initiative	New customers or newly targeted market segment	New investment in digital marketing
Success Factors	**Infrequent users won't need training** Single, comprehensive view of customers Solution grows with changing needs Control over automated response content	Single, comprehensive view of customers Solution grows with changing needs Control over automated response content
Perceived Barriers	Not sure we can trust you Templates require users to know HTML Object to opt-in + first email response Concern about being blacklisted Can't manage another system	Not sure we can trust you Templates require users to know HTML Object to opt-in + first email response Concern about being blacklisted Can't manage another system
Buyer's Journey	**Clients defer decisions to us** We prioritize solutions that we know Expect web access to basic pricing info Need to see/use before I decide Calling to test your responsiveness	**A team evaluates, but I decide** We prioritize solutions that we know Expect web access to basic pricing info Need to see/use before I decide Calling to test your responsiveness
Decision Criteria	**Integrates with most CRM & Web platforms** Works like other software I know, own Lots of easy templates, updated often Easy-to-use automated response	Works like other software I know, own Lots of easy templates, updated often Easy-to-use automated response

Figure 7.3   Is This One or Two Buyer Personas?

persuade these buyers. You can do this by building a table like the one in Figure 7.3 that reflects each of the 21 key Buying Insight headlines from your spreadsheet. The bold type headlines in the agency column are exclusive to agency marketers and the bold insights in the in-house marketing column were voiced exclusively by that segment of buyers. Significantly, there are 15 key Buying Insights, set in a regular typeface, that apply to both audiences.

If your company has a compelling way to address any of the four insights that are unique to agency marketers, or any of the two that are unique to in-house marketers, you have evidence that two buyer personas will help you to win more business. But if the most compelling aspect of your story aligns with the 15 Buying Insights that agency and in-house marketers have in common, you would be better off to create one persona and avoid that additional cost.

For example, if a particular strength of your solution is its ability to integrate with a wide range of Web and customer relationship management (CRM) platforms, you know from your Buying Insights that this attribute will impress the in-house marketer. But marketing campaigns that feature this same attribute are unlikely to resonate with the agency marketer. If in-house marketers represent a large market opportunity and your integration story is far stronger than that presented by your competitors, this finding would absolutely justify a second buyer persona. And it would be reasonable to want to invest in additional research to assure that this is a persistent finding.

On the other hand, if the quality and number of your customizable templates define the most powerful aspect of your solution, you would have no justifiable reason to build two buyer personas. A single, consolidated persona tells the whole story about the Buying Insights that you will need to address.

These two examples of differences in Buying Insights relate directly to observable demographics, but we often find that the differences are better described by other labels. Chapter 9 contains a brief story about the construction equipment manufacturer Caterpillar, Inc., and how their traditional approach to segmentation—defined by the buyer's industry—failed to distinguish useful differences between Buying Insights. Buyer interviews across Caterpillar's target industries, however, reveal differences that merit separate strategies for their "results-oriented" and "detailed-oriented" buyer personas.

Similarly, we have worked on other projects that have defined a company's "ideal" buyer, as differentiated from the "resistant" buyer who has Perceived Barriers that the company cannot overcome. For another client, we found a clearly defined segment of buyers who needed varying degrees of education about the solution before they would even begin to contemplate its value. With this insight the client embarked on marketing strategies for two differing personas: One approach delivered educational material to the uninformed buyer at the appropriate time, while the other approach avoided annoying the buyer with unnecessary educational background and spoke directly to the persona who was ready to assess his or her options.

These are just a few examples of the way distinct patterns in the mind-set of buyers can be labeled to describe the differences between buyer personas. You will want to hone your ability to discern patterns revealed in your Buying Insights and align your personas around descriptive categories reflecting facts most helpful to your marketing team.

It's essential to avoid any premature idea about how many buyer personas you will need. If you define your buyer personas based on the differences in Buyer Profiles, far too many personas will be the result and you will burden your execution team with irrelevant and distracting details. You cannot know how many buyer personas you will need until you complete your buyer interviews, analyze the 5 Rings of Buying Insight, and evaluate whether the differences you discovered justify a differentiated marketing strategy.

Presenting Your Buyer Persona

Once you have completed the Insights Aggregator spreadsheet and determined how many buyer personas you need, your next step is to ensure that you communicate the Buying Insights on your spreadsheet in a format that helps your company align its strategies with what you've learned.

Marketers enjoy a lot of creative options for these presentations. In addition to PowerPoint, we've seen posters, infographics, and elaborate intranet sites where internal teams can find the buyer personas that will help them make decisions. Any or all of these are appropriate, bearing in mind that you want to choose a format that is most helpful to your internal audience, even if it does not earn you any design awards.

We will discuss how to use your buyer personas for strategic and tactical decisions in Part III of the book. For now, however, please resist the urge to celebrate the completion of your buyer persona with a distribution to all employees.

The most common way to present buyer personas is a PowerPoint (PPT) presentation. Figures 7.4–7.9 are examples of the PPT template that we use, completed with the findings for Amanda, the persona we built in Chapter 6. Whatever format you select, your final buyer persona presentation should use verbatim quotations from your Insights Aggregator spreadsheet. You will want to prioritize the quotations and insights that were expressed by multiple buyers, but since this is qualitative research, there is no hard-and-fast rule that determines how many of the people you interviewed need to have the same point of view.

If you conducted a quantitative study to test your interview findings, use your survey results to prioritize the presentation of the key Buying Insights and quotations. Because a follow-up survey is relatively rare, however, we usually give priority to any thoughts that were expressed frequently, and rarely include quotations that were not expressed by at least two people.

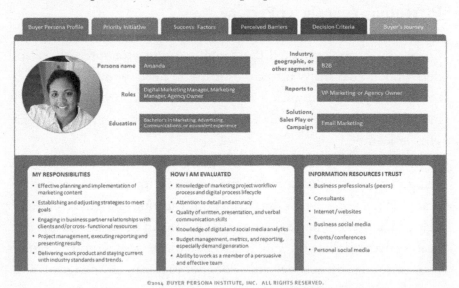

Figure 7.4 Example Buyer Profile

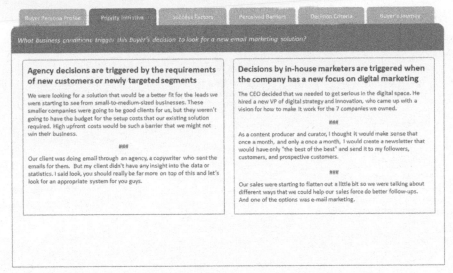

Buyer Persona Profile · **Priority Initiative** · **Success Factors** · **Perceived Barriers** · **Decision Criteria** · **Buyer's Journey**

What business conditions trigger this buyer's decision to look for a new email marketing solution?

Agency decisions are triggered by the requirements of new customers or newly targeted segments

We were looking for a solution that would be a better fit for the leads we were starting to see from small-to-medium-sized businesses. These smaller companies were going to be good clients for us, but they weren't going to have the budget for the setup costs that our existing solution required. High upfront costs would be such a barrier that we might not win their business.

###

Our client was doing email through an agency, a copywriter who sent the emails for them. But my client didn't have any insight into the data or statistics. I said look, you should really be far more on top of this and let's look for an appropriate system for you guys.

Decisions by in-house marketers are triggered when the company has a new focus on digital marketing

The CEO decided that we needed to get serious in the digital space. He hired a new VP of digital strategy and innovation, who came up with a vision for how to make it work for the 7 companies we owned.

###

As a content producer and curator, I thought it would make sense that once a month, and only a once a month, I would create a newsletter that would have only "the best of the best" and send it to my followers, customers, and prospective customers.

###

Our sales were starting to flatten out a little bit so we were talking about different ways that we could help our sales force do better follow-ups. And one of the options was e-mail marketing.

Figure 7.5   Example Priority Initiative Insights

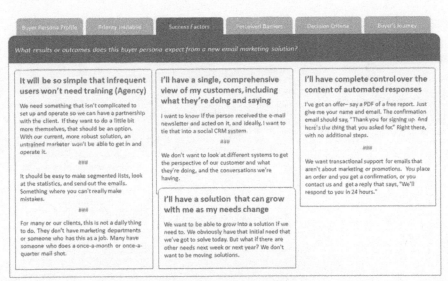

Buyer Persona Profile · **Priority Initiative** · **Success Factors** · **Perceived Barriers** · **Decision Criteria** · **Buyer's Journey**

What results or outcomes does this buyer persona expect from a new email marketing solution?

It will be so simple that infrequent users won't need training (Agency)

We need something that isn't complicated to set up and operate so we can have a partnership with the client. If they want to do a little bit more themselves, that should be an option. With our current, more robust solution, an untrained marketer won't be able to get in and operate it.

###

It should be easy to make segmented lists, look at the statistics, and send out the emails. Something where you can't really make mistakes.

###

For many or our clients, this is not a daily thing to do. They don't have marketing departments or someone who has this as a job. Many have someone who does a once-a-month or once-a-quarter mail shot.

I'll have a single, comprehensive view of my customers, including what they're doing and saying

I want to know if the person received the e-mail newsletter and acted on it, and ideally, I want to tie that into a social CRM system.

###

We don't want to look at different systems to get the perspective of our customer and what they're doing, and the conversations we're having.

I'll have a solution that can grow with me as my needs change

We want to be able to grow into a solution if we need to. We obviously have that initial need that we've got to solve today. But what if there are other needs next week or next year? We don't want to be moving solutions.

I'll have complete control over the content of automated responses

I've got an offer— say a PDF of a free report. Just give me your name and email. The confirmation email should say, "Thank you for signing up. And here's the thing that you asked for." Right there, with no additional steps.

###

We want transactional support for emails that aren't about marketing or promotions. You place an order and you get a confirmation, or you contact us and get a reply that says, "We'll respond to you in 24 hours."

Figure 7.6   Example Success Factors Insights

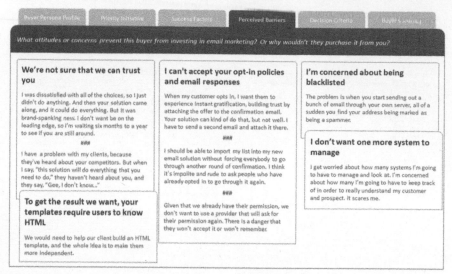

Figure 7.7   Example Perceived Barriers Insights

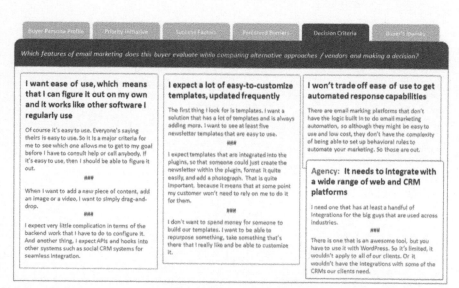

Figure 7.8   Example Decision Criteria Insights

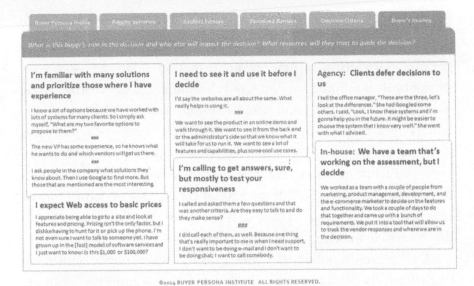

Figure 7.9   Example Buyer's Journey Insights

Copywriting Your Buying Insights

Once you know which buyer quotations will appear in your buyer persona, you'll want to *slightly* edit the verbatim quotations from your interviews to make them more readable. Eliminate repeated words and half-formed phrases. But make sure not to insert your own words, sanitize the quotation, summarize salient points, or eliminate colorful turns of phrase. Your goal is to faithfully report the buyer's words, cogently communicating thoughts and emotions even if the sentence is a copywriter's nightmare.

Next, use your best copywriting skills to help you create your final key Buying Insight headlines. Many stakeholders will scan these headlines without reading the buyer's quotations, so you will want to include as much detail as possible. We've found it useful to follow the organizing format of the spreadsheet with separate pages devoted to each of the 5 Rings of Buying Insight, and to write each headline as if the buyer was directly answering that ring's question. For example, you have a group of related quotations that answer the question that defines Success Factors: "What results or outcomes does this buyer persona expect from a new email marketing solution?" On your spreadsheet you used a shorthand headline to summarize these quotations: "easy, fast, automated communications." However, on your buyer persona presentation page, you want to restate this headline in the voice of a person who is directly answering the Success Factor question. For this group of quotations you might write a headline such as, "I'll have complete control over the content of automated responses." The goal is to create a headline that conveys the core idea with conviction and urgency.

Under each headline you will want to display buyer quotations that effectively communicate specific details that support the headline. In the case earlier, the quotations will explain what it means for the buyer to have control over automated responses. You will be unable to use all of the quotations contained on your spreadsheet, so you should select those that are the most colorful while also watching for any that provide valuable specificity.

Building the Buyer Profile

The Buyer Profile helps you communicate to others which buyers you grouped together when you analyzed your Buying Insights. Most marketers give their Buyer Profiles a proper name and picture, but both are optional. It can be helpful to name the Buyer Profile, so that the buyer persona becomes "real" to internal stakeholders. Additionally among members of a marketing team, when the Buyer Profile name is invoked in conversation, it serves as a short hand that refers to all the Buying Insights associated with that buyer persona. We've seen companies use these names in internal meetings and communications whenever they want to reference the findings contained in the buyer persona.

There are downsides to this practice, however, as we've seen teams waste time on debates about demographics such as the age, gender, and ethnicity of their buyer persona when none of these will have any impact on their marketing strategies. If you think this may be a problem in your company, try to choose a name that is gender neutral and skip the photo.

How to Find Buyer Profile Information

Amanda's profile identifies her various job titles and provides bulleted summaries that describe her responsibilities. You might confirm your buyer's job title during your interviews, but whenever possible you'll want to avoid asking questions where the answers could be obtained through a quick online search. When looking for information on B2B job descriptions and background about years of experience and education, you can access data from the LinkedIn profiles of the people you interviewed.

The information conveyed in the "resources consulted" section of the profile will come from directly from your interviews; you should consolidate the sources buyers referenced when they told you how they evaluated their options. But feel free to supplement your interview findings with any data from surveys, analysts, or other sources with larger sample sizes.

If you want to capture any other profile information during your interviews, reserve any such questions for the end of the interview. As we discussed in Chapter 5, you should aim to engage your buyer in telling his or her story as soon as possible to set the tone for a conversation that enlists the buyer's full attention. Keep any questions that are unrelated to the buyer's story to a bare minimum and ask them only after you have learned everything you can about the decision.

Sometimes it is helpful to use the interview to capture Buyer Profile information that reveals how the buyer's success is measured

within the organization. Another question might ask the buyer
to describe his or her three top priorities during the upcoming
12 months. This aspect of the profile may be helpful as you consider
which of your other solutions would be most likely to capture this
buyer persona's attention in the near term.

As we discussed in Chapter 3, you may have information from
other sources including social media that will help you complete the
Buyer Profile. Just keep in mind that every characteristic you include
should help you make better marketing decisions. Irrelevant information puts your buyer persona initiative at risk with stakeholders who
may view it as foolish or question the need for additional personas.
You should keep your focus on the Buying Insights and ensure that
the Buyer Profile is used to help your team identify people who share
your buyer persona's expectations.

PART III

Aligning Your Strategies to Win More Business

Now that you understand the attributes of useful personas and the methodology to discover Buying Insights, we want to be sure that you have a clear plan to use your insights to guide your marketing decisions. Your buyer personas are a marketing tool—a means and not an end. We hear from marketers every day who are responding to a directive to build buyer personas, but they can't tell us how they will be used.

Harold Geneen, the twentieth-century business executive whom the *New York Times* compared to General George S. Patton, Alexander the Great, and Napoleon, reflected on strategy with these words: "You read a book from beginning to end. You run a business the opposite way. You start with the end, and then you do everything you must to reach it."

We built the buyer persona methodology because we knew precisely what the end result needed to be. Our vision didn't begin with the goal to invent a new research methodology or to understand

131

buyers. Instead, we realized that marketers of high-consideration products needed the insight and confidence to build strategies that would help buyers choose their solution. So we invented a methodology that would provide it.

We've been worried that thousands of marketers may be building ineffective buyer personas, publishing them on their intranet, and then letting them drown in a sea of PowerPoints that no one can recall. So when we saw that Dan Staresinic, a senior marketing executive at one of the world's largest engineering companies, had successfully communicated the value of buyer personas in this memo to his marketing team, we asked for permission to share his communication with you.

Re: Buyer Personas

Everything that I am learning says that our communications group is creating a competitive advantage of significant proportions vs. our competitors. Major outside agencies tell me that we are doing more and achieving faster results with respect to personas than others in our industry. I sat with a panel of local CMOs last week and was the only one of the ten who had any experience implementing personas as a foundation for integrated marketing communication planning and execution.

And we have the evidence that it works. Here are the results of one product team chosen at random: In the twelve months prior to going live with their persona-based campaign, they generated something like 90 hot leads, most of which were not, in fact, so hot. In the two-and-a-half months since turning the campaign on, they have generated more than 50 hot leads, all of which are verifiably hot. That is a salesperson's dream. It eventually becomes a shareholder's dream. To be clear, it is more than personas that deliver this result. It is a smart, integrated campaign that incorporates many best practices. But it would be just another campaign that produced typical results if not for its underpinning of deeply insightful personas.

I have concluded that nobody among our close competitive set is fully exploiting the operational difference between purely demographic personas (the kind you can make by collecting information from LinkedIn profiles and extrapolating liberally) and personas based on deep, time-consuming research. But they will figure it out sooner or later.

It is therefore my hope that each of you will become a qualified persona interviewer and will immediately put your new skill into regular practice. I urge each of you to adopt a personal objective today to conduct at least one persona interview per month (though the more you can do, the better you and our company will be) and to ensure that the wisdom that you document continuously finds its way into our persona library.

Our strategy must be to push this advantage forward as forcefully and rapidly as our system can effectively bear. That is where we all must count on you. You will soon possess advanced knowledge and skills in this area. You must stand up if we are not doing the right thing. You must develop your own credible point of view on the value of deeply insightful personas and back that up with your own evidence. And, using that, you must convert this organization into one that makes all of its important marketing communication decisions based on deeply insightful personas.

Thank you for making the commitment to acquiring these new skills and for your efforts to use them to drive improved outcomes.

Clearly, there are C-suite executives who are exploiting buyer persona insight for competitive advantages, focused messaging, and other initiatives. As of this writing, however, we cannot point to any one company that is doing everything we'll cover in the chapters to come. So take heart, it is not necessary to accomplish all of these changes to see benefits from your buyer personas.

In fact, we recommend marketers choose only one place to begin to work with buyer personas, a topic we will cover in the final chapter. Even if all of your buyer personas could suddenly appear with the wave of a magic wand, you will not see any of their benefits unless you are willing to take direction from them.

In the pages that follow we'll show you how some companies are using buyer personas to make decisions that have helped them win more business. Then we'll consider the implications that buyer personas suggest for changing the way business is conducted going forward, as organizations incorporate the voice of the buyer into many crucial decisions—and marketing gains a new respected authority.

8

Decide What to Say to Buyers

In 2008, Linda Stone, a former Apple and Microsoft executive, coined the term *continuous partial attention* (CPA) to describe an increasingly pervasive mental state unique to the digital age. Stone defined CPA as the state of mind that people experience as they try to pay attention to multiple sources of information. The desire to optimize opportunities and maintain human connections has always been a fundamental aspect of humanity, but our "always on, anywhere, anytime" environment has ratcheted up the stakes.

Catching someone's attention and being heard amid this streaming torrent of information is the greatest challenge of contemporary marketing. The buyers we need to persuade are navigating an overwhelming flood of information, rapidly processing and eliminating anything that doesn't instantly connect with their priorities and expectations. That ever-present "x" button is our biggest threat as buyers quickly delete any email and close any document that doesn't tell them something that clearly delivers value.

Fully 60 to 70 percent of content churned out by business-to-business (B2B) marketing departments today sits unused.
—Reported in a 2013 SiriusDecisions Survey

Will Your Current Approach Work?

Against this backdrop we can begin to see the futility of traditional approaches for choosing the words and topics that engage buyers. Whether selecting themes for an important campaign, preparing for an upcoming launch, or planning for a major event, those who are trying to influence buyers are probably quite knowledgeable about the value delivered by your product or service as well as your company's goals.

Working alone or in a meeting with these experts, such initiatives often begin by concentrating on the people you want to influence, imagining their goals, and focusing on statements describing the benefits of your approach. Product experts tend to explain how the new functionality will help companies to grow their business, increase operational efficiency, or reduce costs. An expert on the competition may contribute points about why your solution is superior. Someone else describes the need to educate buyers about your company's vision to address an emerging market trend.

This approach to message development is so commonplace that marketers don't notice that they are attempting to build buyer-focused messaging in a setting where the buyer's perspective is unrepresented. Sure, everyone is thinking about the buyer as they convert features to benefits, focusing on the results your solution delivers rather than its capabilities. But it's unlikely that anyone participating in this exercise can say, for example, that your buyer already knows that a customer relationship management solution will help them to deliver personalized, targeted marketing campaigns.

Will anyone have the confidence to inform the meeting that the chief marketing officer is far more interested in hearing about how the dashboard can be customized to display views that address the needs of very different types of users? And who can defend the need for this specificity when the detractors note that this is a feature, and that the message must instead focus on the benefit of monitoring marketing return on investment (ROI)?

Your messaging decisions must take into account your company's goal to communicate the value of its solutions as well as your buyer's attitudes, needs, and concerns. Through the lens of the 5 Rings of Buying Insight, you have a tool to bring your buyer's authentic voice to bear on the messaging decision.

In their interviews, your buyers described their Priority Initiative or the business triggers that caused them to abandon the status quo and become interested in investing in a solution. Their Success Factors described the benefits that motivated this investment. You know about the negative perceptions or obstacles that your message needs to address from the Perceived Barriers insight, and in the Decision Criteria insight, you have confirmation that they indeed want to hear about certain features and capabilities.

These insights mean that among the many features, capabilities, and benefits discussed by the product managers and experts, we can readily isolate those that will engage particular buyers and interest them in learning more.

In many actual case studies, we've seen new features that were considered relatively unimportant to buyers, especially during the early stages of their buying journey. In other instances there were features that the company had taken for granted that were, in fact, the most compelling way to engage select audiences.

We've also seen features, capabilities, and benefits that appear irrelevant to buyers that nevertheless provide huge value. Having never considered a need for such capabilities, buyers don't focus on these during their search and evaluation. This doesn't mean that we won't include this information in our messaging. However, we need to initiate communication with buyers by addressing their primary concerns, and once they are engaged, we can then introduce additional educational information that positions our approach.

Your direction is simple: Effective messaging emerges at the intersection of what your buyers want to hear and what you want to say. Some companies can find this sweet spot by adjusting their current messaging with the addition of buyer persona insights.

Many companies, however, need to entirely rethink their approach to messaging decisions. In the event that you're in the latter category, here is a methodology that assures success.

Set the Agenda, and Invite the Right People

Calling for a messaging strategy meeting follows the same triggering events that prompted the meeting described earlier—typically a launch or revised campaign that involves new marketing materials. Or it may be that you have just completed a buyer persona and gained an insight that suggests a midcourse correction to an existing messaging strategy.

The meeting's objective is to define and choose the content that will appear in the product, service, or solution messaging. However, because copywriting is an art form that should never be done by committee, no writing of actual copy will be done at the meeting. (Professionals will execute it later.) Here the objective is to carefully evaluate and select what we want the message to convey, without wrangling over the precise wording.

Participants at the meeting will include those who generally attend messaging strategy meetings at your company—they usually call on the knowledge of a solution expert as well as someone who knows the competitive landscape.

You will also want to include at least one person who is going to execute the messaging, write the website content, or compose the white paper. It's important that they understand how and why the messaging content was chosen.

Finally, you will need a moderator whose central role will be to represent the authentic voice of the buyer persona. When the discussion begins to focus on the appeal and importance of a particular capability, the moderator/buyer persona expert is available to articulate whether it is among the buyer's concerns.

Ideally, you want no more than four to six participants; any more than this number makes it difficult to arrive at conclusions. Should it be necessary to include others, it's best to limit their participation as observers.

The messaging strategy will be done in two parts, usually on two separate days. You will probably need about three hours for each meeting. Here is the recommended agenda for each of the meetings:

Day 1: Find the intersection between what you want to say and what the buyer wants to hear. At the end of this meeting you will have anywhere from 20 to 30 or more topics that you will want to feature in your "long form" content (e.g., white papers, ebooks, or articles) or "recurring" messaging (e.g., blogs, newsletters, or social media).

Day 2: Develop your short messaging by applying two filters to the list you created on Day 1. At the end of this meeting, you will have five bullet points plus the content of your short positioning statement or elevator pitch.

Let's look at how you might run these meetings.

Ask for Premeeting Contributions

Before the meeting, the moderator should request that each participant prepare a bulleted list that describes the aspects of the solution he or she considers the most valuable in the eyes of the buyer. Each person should produce a list of no more than 10 points. They needn't be carefully crafted or perfectly written, and they shouldn't be created in collaboration. The objective is for each participant to list the points that he or she believes are important.

Potentially, if you have six participants and each submits a list of 10 items, you might have as many as 60 bullet points. Because there will be some degree of overlap, it will be the moderator's responsibility to organize and consolidate these submissions into general topic areas. Since this is only a quest for content, not precise language, the wording isn't crucial. This completed list is a draft of "what we want to say" about this solution. As we work through this chapter, we'll call this the Capabilities List.

Next, to create a bulleted list of "What the buyer wants to hear" the moderator will copy the key Buying Insight headlines from the buyer persona—focusing on the Priority Initiatives, Success Factors, Decision Criteria, and Perceived Barrier insights. (The moderator need not reference the Buyer's Journey insights as these are unlikely to impact marketing messaging. We'll be working with the Buyer's Journey insights in Chapter 9.)

To make it easy to refer to these 16 to 20 headlines, we'll call this list your Buyer's Expectations.

Each of the participants will need to have both of these lists—the Capabilities List and Buyer's Expectations—in addition to the full buyer persona to reference during the meeting.

Develop a Complete List of Capabilities That Matter

Start the first meeting by asking the participants to look at the bulleted list of Buyer's Expectations to see if it contains anything that your solution can't deliver. If you don't have any way to address one of your buyer's needs, that point will not be featured in your messaging. You will want to use this insight later for sales enablement, which we'll discuss in Chapter 10, but you should eliminate it from the working list for this meeting.

Next, taking the two lists and working with them side-by-side, go through the Buyer's Expectations one at a time, referencing the Capabilities List to find statements that describe or prove your company's ability to address that need.

Whenever a bullet point on the list of Buyer's Expectations comes up for discussion, the moderator should ensure that the team fully understands the need by reading the verbatim quotations from the buyer persona. The moderator should use the voice of the buyer to encourage the participants to fully consider the buyer's mind-set and the details of the buyer's expectations. This focus on the specific, detailed insights discovered during the buyer interviews is the team's first step toward eliminating conventional, generic, and jargon-laden messages.

For instance, consider a marketing team that's aware that buyers are reluctant to invest in solutions that might become obsolete in a few years, a Perceived Barriers insight. Wanting to counter that concern, the participants first suggested this bullet point on their Capabilities List: "We have the flexibility to design a solution that meets your needs now and in the future."

The moderator, speaking for the buyer, reminds the team that merely telling buyers that the company has addressed this concern is insufficient. Buyers are completing 60 percent of the decision process using information found online, and their continuous partial attention means that they aren't going to read anything that isn't helpful. The moderator insists that the team needs bullet points that address the buyers' specific expectations related to "flexible designs."

To enable a meaningful discussion, the team turns back to the buyer persona to see if flexibility was among the buyer's Decision Criteria. If it's there, quotations from the buyer interview will explain that flexibility is about adapting to evolving industry standards and a range of technology platforms.

The Moderator Is a Proxy for the Buyer

Companies are often surprised that it takes a full three hours (and sometimes longer) to find the intersection between their Capabilities List and the list of Buyer's Expectations. This process will get easier as the participants become accustomed to working with buyer personas, but the first time through this process is difficult for most marketers. It usually takes time for marketers to think about how they can provide clear and convincing evidence that they can meet their buyer's specific expectations.

The meeting moderator will likely need to interrupt the automatic thinking that usually results in stale, timeworn summary messages about the awesome benefits delivered by the solution under discussion. The moderator will need to point out that the buyer persona knows about these benefits (referencing the Success Factors insight) and that the meeting needs to focus on persuading the buyer that the company can deliver the capabilities that produce these results.

As your team works through the Capabilities List, remind them that they need not worry about the number of bullet points or expend effort trying to make them pithy and concise. The job for this team is to fully articulate any capabilities that the buyer will find relevant and helpful.

This discussion works only if the moderator can actively field questions, provide answers, or interject comments that speak in the voice of the buyer persona. Some will even speak as a proxy for the buyer, pressing participants to expand on their messaging by asking questions such as, "Can you be more specific so that your message directly addresses my concerns? Otherwise I'm going to look elsewhere." If a messaging suggestion is too general or doesn't sound convincing to the buyer persona, the moderator should counter, "That's not persuasive to me. I don't believe you."

Members of the marketing team can then respond to the moderator/ buyer persona with questions such as, "We want our copy to emphasize that our solution is relatively easy to use, but I get the impression you want to hear much more than that. What exactly do you need to hear from us that will convince you of that fact?"

When the messaging is refined to include the details the buyer is seeking, the moderator may reinforce the process in the buyer's voice by interjecting, "Wow! This is great. This is precisely what I am looking for."

As a final part of this first step, look at your premeeting Capabilities List to see if everything that seemed important to the participants has been matched to one of your Buyer's Expectations. If anything essential remains on that list, you may want to review your results to see if there is a place where that capability applies. If that isn't possible and you have an "orphan" capability from the first day's session, you'll learn how to use that insight in the Thought Leadership section of Chapter 9 as well as in Chapter 10's discussion on Sales Enablement.

At the end of the first day's meeting you may have one, two, or perhaps three compelling bullet points that directly address each of your Buyer's Expectations—capabilities that tell the buyer that your approach to solving the problem is an ideal match for the buyer's needs. In Chapter 9, we will explore the steps your team will take to communicate every one of these points through a range of marketing activities.

First, let's look at the second part of your Messaging Strategy Meeting, where you will develop a shorter version of this message.

Apply Two Filters for Short Messaging

There will be many times when you have only a few seconds or a minute to capture your buyer persona's attention and persuade the buyer to take the next step to consider you. This is one of the most challenging steps in messaging because either you will have to choose which of the salient points to communicate, or you will have to create a summary that conveys several points at once. Most marketers choose the summary approach for short messaging because no one knows which of the statements will have the desired effect. Alas, this shotgun approach tends to produce messaging that buyers describe as generic and irrelevant, such as, "We are the market-leading supplier of flexible, scalable, compatible, enterprise-wide [insert widget category here]." All gobbledygook, but I confess, I've agreed to the use of these exact words in many messages. After several hours of sitting in a room trying to make up a message guided only by the opinions of the people in that room, I'll agree to anything. Just let me outta there!

Now that you have listened to buyers relate their stories detailing how they make their choices, you have insight into the practical and emotional aspects of your buyer's decision. You can avoid writing summaries for short-form messaging and choose the specific points that will have the most impact on the buyer's decision. Imagine the buyer's reaction when, unlike your competitors' messages, your message communicates your ability to address one of the buyer's most cherished expectations.

We recommend that you apply two filters to the first day's Capabilities List to help you decide which of these points achieves this goal. For the first filter, you will evaluate each statement based on your competitors' ability to make that statement. The second filter requires your team to rank the capabilities based on their relative importance to your buyers.

Evaluate Your Competitive Ranking

Working with each of the bullet points on the Capabilities List you developed during the first day of your Messaging Strategy Meeting, the participants will work together to assign one of the following numerical values to each statement:

1. *Impossible:* Your competitors cannot claim this capability. (Be careful, this is rare.)
2. *Difficult:* Your competitors can make this claim, but if you have a chance to tell your full story, you can clearly demonstrate your superiority.
3. *Easy:* Your competitors can readily match this capability.

Naturally, these rankings will require some intelligence about the competition and are likely to vary for each competitor. Don't worry too much about that part of the discussion because our objective isn't a precise measurement. We are interested only in an indicator about the relative strength and weakness of the claim.

An important side effect of assigning these Competitive Rankings is that it encourages the team to adjust the content of their first meeting's Capability List statements. When people see that their generic statements result in too many Competitive Rankings of "three," they are highly motivated to revise the statement to say something more compelling and specific.

Using the sort feature on your spreadsheet, you can easily see the capability statements with the highest Competitive Ranking (1) at the top, and the weakest (3) at the bottom of your list.

Assess Relative Value to Buyers

Although the step you just completed reveals your competitive advantages in terms of their singularity, it doesn't tell you which of your capabilities is most important to your buyers. We want to consider competitive advantages as one aspect of choosing your messaging, while avoiding those unfortunate situations where the company emphasizes a unique aspect of their solution that has little or no effect on the buyer's decision.

We eliminated the risk that you will say anything that is completely irrelevant to your buyer by working from a list of Buyer's Expectations at the start of this process. But because this step will result in a short message used to initially engage the buyer, in this final step you want to identify the capabilities that most effectively address your buyer's urgent or compelling expectations.

To complete this assessment, the meeting participants need to rank the capabilities based on their relative ability to affect your buyer's decision. Doing so usually requires the participants to make a judgment call. This is accomplished by reviewing verbatim quotations in the buyer persona and finding statements that evoke vivid or emotional reactions. Then, with the buyer in mind, evaluate each capability to determine how well it communicates value to the persona.

For companies wanting a greater degree of confidence that their short message is ideal, testing it with a survey or a focus group often provides the assurance that it was chosen wisely. As discussed in Chapter 5, a few companies exercise the option to conduct quantitative research following buyer interviews in order to validate a buyer persona. If so, this study may have already resulted in a hierarchical list of Buyer's Expectations.

Because most companies rely on judgment to develop this ranking, however, for our example we'll let the participants at the Messaging Strategy Meeting make this decision. Working as a team, they rank each capability either A, B, or C. An A ranking designates a capability included in messaging that the buyer will find of highest value, whereas B and C rankings apply to those that are likely to have relatively less impact.

The moderator's role is to help the participants evaluate each capability statement from two perspectives: How much urgency does the buyer assign to this expectation, and how well does your statement communicate your ability to deliver what your buyer expects?

Once you have assigned these rankings, sort your list a final time. At the top of the list you will see those capabilities that communicate the most value to your buyers; those that have lesser value will appear in the middle, and those with the least value will fall to the bottom.

If you are lucky, you will see that a few of the capabilities at the top of your list also have high Competitive Rankings. But don't be surprised if that doesn't happen. In Table 8.1 you can see that the statements with the most value to buyers earned a Competitive Ranking of 2. Competitors can make these same statements, but when marketers or salespeople have a chance to present a long form of their message, they can prove their approach is superior.

We've also seen instances where a message that ranked highest on the list of value to buyers earned only a Competitive Ranking of 3. In one memorable case, a company that will remain unnamed here shipped a solution that had a number of flaws. As one of the largest suppliers in this category, this problem was highly visible to the company's prospective customers. When they initiated their Messaging Strategy Meeting they had resolved the problem and added new, differentiated capabilities that they fully expected to feature in their upcoming launch. However, by working through this process they realized their folly. The new capability barely registered as a Buyer's Expectation. Instead, at the top of the list of value to buyers was concern about the emotional fallout that came as a consequence of the flawed release. This had been discovered during buyer interviews and appeared in the buyer persona as a Perceived Barriers insight. The product team that had worked so hard on the new features resisted the creation of messaging that didn't emphasize their contribution. The senior executives and salespeople, however, applauded the marketing team's decision to speak directly to what mattered most to their buyers.

Table 8.1 Example Messaging Strategy Final Ranking

Source of Expectation	High–Value Capabilities	Competitive Ranking	Relative Importance to Buyer
Priority Initiative	Integra's 99 percent customer retention rate is proof of our competitive, cost-effective solutions and commitment to nurturing a long-term partnership. We don't just sell something and walk away.	1	A
Success Factors	Integra's security portfolio includes Professional Services, DDoS mitigation, and firewall service to ensure your network is protected 360 degrees. Integra will partner with you to develop robust business continuity disaster recovery solutions to ensure your business is always operational with a secure, redundant network delivered over a private Ethernet connection. (Emphasize Magic Quadrant leading partners covering all layers of your network.)	2	A

Table 8.1 (continued)

Source of Expectation	High-Value Capabilities	Competitive Ranking	Relative Importance to Buyer
Success Factors	Integra owns and operates an enterprise-class network, designed to support the needs of business migrating to the cloud to reduce CapEx and improve efficiency with up to 100 Gbps connections optimized for high capacity and low latency; to partnerships with cloud providers. Emphasis on hands-on migration process and full migration plan.	3	A
Perceived Barriers	Integra is a local technology company with a national presence delivering managed services and IP/MPLS networks to every major metropolitan area in the United States.	2	A
Perceived Barriers and Decision Criteria	Design for now and the future: Integra account specialists consult/partner with you to design the right solution architecture as your business grows. You won't be shoehorned into a less than ideal solution because we have all options available, every architectural capability—from high-bandwidth wavelength and Ethernet services to IP/MPLS VPN solutions and a full-range of VoIP (or IP telephony) options.	2	A

Bring in the Copywriters and Creative Teams

As a result of these meetings you have a collection of capability statements that convey the information your buyers want to hear. You've sorted the list to ensure that you put the greatest emphasis on the capabilities that are most likely to persuade buyers, based on a combination of their competitive rankings as well as their relative value in the eyes of the buyer.

Now it's time to write the final copy. If you have the resources to employ a creative team or external resource, give them your buyer persona and the final spreadsheet you built during your Messaging Strategy Meeting. Be prepared to explain what you learned and how you made your decisions. If you chose well this won't take long, and soon their heads will nod in agreement as they realize you've already done a lot of hard work for them. They should understand how your insights and strategy will help them be truly effective.

If you are writing your own copy, we won't attempt to teach you how in these pages. We refer instead to others who have great advice on this topic. See especially Ann Handley's well-reviewed book *Everyone Writes*.

However, we will ask you to ensure that whoever writes the final version of your message retains the specificity that you worked so hard to identify. Don't allow summaries, superlatives, and other forms of drivel to cloud your ability to speak directly and clearly. You and your team have invested time and effort interviewing buyers and carefully analyzing their responses to obtain Buying Insights. You have defined the intersection between what you have to say and what your buyers want to hear. Unless you have a huge budget to spend on branding a message, such as Nike's "Just Do It," your message needs to speak plainly and simply. It should help buyers like those in your buyer persona discover that your approach is an ideal fit for their needs. Stay firmly focused on that goal, and you'll make good decisions.

9 | Design Marketing Activities to Enable Your Buyer's Journey

When you think about the best way to engage your buyers, you are likely to be confronted by a bewildering variety of options. In his book *Youtility*, digital marketing strategist and best-selling author Jay Baer suggests some simple but surprising guidance to anyone facing this quandary: "Your marketing should be so useful that people would gladly pay for it."

We are not suggesting that your buyers should offer their VISA card information in exchange for your white paper or webinar. Rather that this value is one of the standards you should apply to every marketing decision. Focus on designing your lead generation campaign to make it more useful to your buyers.

Should you offer an extremely valuable asset before you ask your buyers to "pay" with their name and email address? Or should you forego the registration until you have given your buyers something useful for free? Would you describe yourself as the market-leading provider of flexible, scalable, compatible, easy-to-use widgets if you

151

wanted to help your buyers evaluate your solution's applicability for their needs?

The perfect time to be useful begins when your buyer decides to prioritize an investment in a solution much like the one you are offering. At this moment, you don't have to be pushy or particularly clever to gain attention. Now your buyer is looking for the information to determine your ability to address his or her requirements.

If you have done your buyer interviews, you know that this buyer persona has a specific goal—your Priority Initiative insight—and is doing considerable work to understand who is best qualified to deliver on expectations—Success Factors, Perceived Barriers, and Decision Criteria insights. Even if your solution is more expensive, you can earn your buyers' trust by delivering the answers they want to hear through the resources they trust—revealed in your Buyer's Journey insight. One of the most important uses of your buyer persona is to help you deliver the useful marketing content that makes this assessment easy for your buyers.

Ideally, you don't want to wait until the moment of need to market to your buyer. We'll address that situation later in this chapter. First, however, let's establish that your most urgent goal is to be useful to people at the moment they are researching and asking questions about solutions like the one you offer. Buyers at this stage of their journey will make their decision far sooner than those who aren't yet looking. Accordingly, this comprises the shortest pathway from insights to leads and revenue. If that isn't motivation enough, consider the implications if you mount a successful effort to bring people into the top of your sales funnel and then disappoint them once they begin to engage with you.

When you understand your buyer persona and focus on creating useful information, you create the trust that inspires buyers to initiate a relationship with you. As Jay Baer says, "There are two ways for companies to succeed in this era: Be amazing or be useful. The latter is much more reliable and viable."

Understand the Buyer's Journey

The commonly existing confusion about the definition of buyer personas and the manner in which they are constructed extends equally to the concept of the Buyer's Journey. This misinformation is fueled by countless blog posts and articles describing the journey as a funnel, a maze, and, of greatest concern, a highly structured process where buyers consume long lists of marketing assets at every step of their decision.

Conduct a Google search on "Buyer's Journey" and you'll find a dizzying array of images and posts defining the steps in the journey or the questions that buyers ask at each step. A few people even purport to identify the marketing assets that you need to build to motivate buyers at each stage of their decision.

This is another version of the guesswork that is asked of you when your buyer personas don't include Buying Insights. The interview-based Buyer's Journey is intended to help you build a strategy that will persuade the most influential buyers and defend your plan even when it entails unexpected investments. More critically, it should give you the credibility to eliminate an idea that is a waste of time and expenses, no matter where that idea originated.

At the 2014 Content Marketing World Conference, Kristina Halvorson said that most marketers operate without anything she would describe as a strategy, noting that we misuse the word unless our plan helps us focus on a specific goal, prioritize the best ideas, and exclude those that make no sense. The audience responded with guilty laughter as Halvorson showed examples of marketing that would never have seen the light of day had their strategy defined the needs of the audience, established constraints, and helped the team "say no" to dumb stuff.

When you interview your buyers, you will discover that the reality of your Buyer's Journey differs greatly from online depictions. For example, you will find that their journey varies significantly according to the nature of their decision.

You can see this for yourself with your own buying decisions. If you have ever been responsible for choosing the venue for your company's annual customer conference, you will recall that your journey differed significantly from your participation in the selection of a new marketing automation solution. In contrast, consider the path you took when evaluating a new car. These are three very different decisions with three very different journeys. Different stakeholders were involved in each decision, and your personal influence over the outcome varied. Additionally, other than an obvious consultation with your peers, you likely consulted very different resources when searching for guidance.

The idea that you can simply download a template for your Buyer's Journey from the Internet and fill in the relevant details is simply incorrect. If you want to know how your buyers make decisions, you need to ask them to tell you their story.

Patrick's Journey for an Employee Benefits Decision

The strategic value of your Buyer's Journey insight is maximized when you build it in the context of the buying decision you want to influence. In the following example, our buyer persona is an executive named Patrick. From your interviews, you know that Patrick attends a big Human Resources conference where presentations suggest to Patrick that a new approach to employee reviews might reduce turnover—a key success metric identified in Patrick's Buyer Profile.

Over the next year, Patrick sees several related articles in one of the LinkedIn groups that he frequents and decides to consider this investment for the coming budget year. To understand his options, he conducts online research at HR forums to read what his peers are saying about this new approach and speaks directly to a few of them about their experiences. That research gives Patrick a general idea about the initiative's benefits (and risks) as well as the budget he'll need to allocate. Using this information, Patrick builds a minibusiness case and submits it to his boss, the chief human resources officer. In response, he is told to do some further research and follow up when he has a recommendation.

At this point Patrick has selected several promising solution providers and takes the effort to visit each of their websites to learn more. Based on what he discovers online, Patrick eliminates all but two of the companies. (Patrick's Success Factors, Perceived Barriers, and Decision Criteria insights indicate why he decides that the other solution providers can't help him.)

As Patrick's journey continues, he contacts the two remaining providers and requests they deliver an online presentation of their approach. Patrick invites a few of his company's senior business executives to the presentations, including sales and operations because they have expressed concern about employee turnover.

Following up after presentations, sales reps from both companies send product information and customer success stories. Patrick merely glances at the written materials; he's ready to make a decision based on what he's learned during the demo. He explained what he liked and what he didn't like about each solution, and his reactions are captured in his buyer persona Decision Criteria and Perceived Barriers insights. He also indicated that the vice president (VP) of sales thinks one of the solutions is clearly superior, while operations prefers the other for reasons that are captured in the Perceived Barrier and Success Factor insights.

Shortly after the demo, Patrick chooses the solution that he and the sales VP like best and meets with the winning company's sales-person to prepare a business case for the investment. Once completed, Patrick presents the case in a short meeting with his boss, who approves of his decision.

Figure 9.1 is a graphic representation of Patrick's Buyer's Journey.

Buying Process Step	Key Buyer Persona	Other Buyer Personas	Key Rings of Insights	Resources Buyers Consult
Trigger	VP of HR	none	Reduce employee turnover	Conferences, LinkedIn groups
Assess Pros and Cons	VP of HR	CHRO	Risk/benefit analysis, budget	Peers, online research
Research Suppliers	VP of HR	none	See Success Factors, Perceived Barriers, and Decision Criteria Insights	Website research
Evaluate Suppliers	VP of HR	VP of Sales & VP of Ops	See Success Factors, Perceived Barriers, and Decision Criteria Insights	Demo (case studies + datasheets weren't helpful)
Approve Decision	CHRO	VP of HR	CHRO approves solution recommended by VP	None

Figure 9.1   Example Buyer's Journey

Prioritize Assets That Align with the Buyer's Journey

We've seen solution marketers who build and maintain upward of 200 assets for each of their solutions. The Buyer's Journey is extremely valuable in its capability to help the marketing team prioritize their activities and deliverables, and thus reduce that large number of assets dramatically.

It is easy to see how the Buyer's Journey helps the marketing team focus on the assets that will have the most impact on Patrick's decision to purchase an employee benefits solution. Noting that Patrick learns about these solutions through conference attendance and LinkedIn groups, these marketers are giving priority to speaking engagements, conference sponsorships, and participation in those groups.

The Buying Insights indicate that Patrick is heavily influenced by peer input during the research phase, so the team will closely monitor social media, user forums, and customer service records for early warning of any downturn in customer satisfaction or brand reputation.

Reflecting on Patrick's visits to vendor websites and what he told them about his Success Factors and Decision Criteria, they have decided to prominently feature analyst reports, educational videos, and compelling employee retention studies on their site.

To enable the salespeople to excel in the crucial demo phase, the team will build a sales playbook that communicates their insights about Patrick and their strategy to address the VP of operations' Perceived Barriers. (More about this in Chapter 10.)

They will also update their demos and PowerPoint presentation to focus on the Success Factors and Decision Criteria that are critical to Patrick and the other influencers, the VPs of sales and operations. They will slightly rewrite their case studies to ensure that the most compelling aspects of their message are communicated in the first few paragraphs. Finally, they will review their business case template to make sure it includes the elements that Patrick identified as important to his boss.

Rather than developing a standard set of marketing tools for every solution, the Buyer's Journey gave these marketers the confidence to prioritize assets that are helpful for their buyers and salespeople. They learned that the other solutions they market to Patrick require different marketing activities, so they decided to continue to align their internal teams by solution. They know that stakeholders such as sales and customer service will require other deliverables and that this list will grow, but their assessment of Patrick's Buyer's Journey substantially reduced their workload.

Prepare to Be Surprised

Don't make the mistaken assumption that Patrick's journey can speak for the experience of all of your buyers. We have conducted countless interviews and know that every Buyer's Journey has something new to tell us. In one instance, we completed a buyer persona that directly contradicted the widely reported finding that buyers complete at least 60 percent of their decision before they contact salespeople. When faced with the specific decision we evaluated, this particular buyer persona consistently asks each of several suppliers' salespeople to meet with him at the beginning of his search. Why this approach? By meeting with each of these reps during the initial search, he learns about the full range of capabilities that are available to him. Then, with his colleagues, he begins to evaluate his options.

Readers focused on search engine optimization (SEO) should note that although buyers routinely conduct a Google search to see if they've missed any companies they might need to include, the Buyer's Journey for high-consideration decisions seldom indicates that the winning company was found through a Web search during the research phase. In such high-stakes decisions, it appears buyers need to know the company well before their journey begins. The knowledge comes either through their own exposure or through that of a peer. Although SEO is certainly important, it's best to establish Web relationships before the Buyer's Journey actually begins.

When buyers mention that they conducted a Google search, they can be almost apologetic about doing research this way, as if they are confessing to something unprofessional. Unfortunately, buyers can never recall the precise search phrases they used during their online research. Buyer interviews can deliver many insights, but rarely this one.

We can think of only one universal finding about the Buyer's Journey: Everyone consults with their peers. Some meet face-to-face through local networking groups or at conferences, many network online, and others use the telephone. But you can be fairly confident that peer references will affect your inclusion (or exclusion) on the list of suppliers buyers choose to evaluate.

Ultimately, the Buyer's Journey is an uncharted map that you discover by listening to your buyers' stories.

How Buyer Personas Affect Industry or Solution Marketing

If you are responsible for industry-specific strategies for your company, you have likely wondered if you need different buyer personas for each of these vertical segments. Our buyer interviews suggest that going to market by industry is a very important advantage for the companies that have the resources to do so. In interview after interview, buyers report that working with a company that specializes in their industry is among their top Decision Criteria. With a few exceptions, though, including higher education and the public sector, we rarely find that industry is the most useful way to define our clients' buyer personas.

In one recent example the building construction group of Caterpillar asked us to create buyer personas for customers of their compact and small Cat equipment. The marketing team focused on small business owners in five industry segments: residential and commercial construction, concrete construction, agriculture, landscape, and snow and ice removal.

Based on interviews in each of these industries, we discovered all 5 Rings of Buying Insight and found several differences in their buyers' expectations. However, just a few insights revealed that Caterpillar could engage in persuasive, useful marketing efforts by focusing on two buyer personas that span all industries.

One we named the "high-detail persona." These buyers have years, even decades, of experience with heavy equipment. They come to this decision with long lists of specifications for the machines they hope to purchase, and expect that they will have to make compromises, as no one machine is likely to include everything they want. These high-detail buyers want to do side-by-side comparisons of different models of Caterpillar equipment and, ideally, those of the competitors so that they can weigh their options and make those trade-offs.

The second buyer is the "results-oriented persona." These buyers are searching for a new machine that will allow them to do a type of work as they grow their business. Results-oriented persona buyers have little or no experience with the kind of equipment they need and want someone to help them understand their options. They want to be able to reach a knowledgeable distributor on demand, reaching someone they can trust to recommend the machine that is best suited for their needs.

Although these two personas are common across all five of Caterpillar's existing market segments, no one even considered the possibility that Caterpillar should stop producing marketing materials with industry-specific photos. The construction industry buyer wouldn't want to see a landscape photo on a specification sheet, and vice versa.

We've seen similar results when companies evaluate their buyers based on the size of their companies. There are certainly differences in the Buyer's Journey for large enterprises and small businesses, for example. But often the lines of demarcation don't match those our clients were using prior to the study. It appears that these segments are often aligned with the sales organization's territories and channels, rather than meaningful differences in the attributes that guide effective marketing decisions.

As we discussed in Chapter 7, if you market by industry or customer size, it's likely your marketing decisions can be guided by fewer buyer personas than you expect. Once you discover the 5 Rings of Buying Insight, you will know whether your current segments are relevant to your buyer personas and how many you will need.

A Global Perspective on Buyer Personas and Campaigns

Introduce buyer personas into a global company, and you will inevitably hear questions asking whether the insights are consistent across continents. These concerns are sometimes valid, as demonstrated by our stories in Chapter 1 about the failed iPhone 4 launch in Japan and the success achieved by Beko, the Turkish company that adapted their clothes dryers to the expectations of their Chinese customers. However, we see many situations, especially in companies that market high-consideration solutions to technology buyers, where geographic differences are far less significant.

Recently, a well-known global corporation with close to a thousand marketers in offices in more than 100 countries addressed this very situation. Their challenge? While a team based in the United States was building messages and campaigns for the international regions to execute locally, 80 percent of the marketing dollars allocated to each country were being spent creating materials exclusive to that region. The company wanted to eliminate the unnecessary expense and operational inefficiencies, of course. But they also worried that their geographically distributed customers, many of whom worked together to make a buying decision, were being confused by different versions of the company's story.

The company knew that marketers in their regional offices lacked confidence that the campaigns developed in the United States would resonate with their buyers.

The company devised an interesting plan to use buyer personas to resolve this dilemma. Rather than conducting buyer persona research in each geographic region—a solution that would have been prohibitively expensive and time consuming—the company interviewed buyers who worked in the North American offices of their global customers. Then, based on their buyer persona insights, the team created messages and campaign materials that could be delivered through a wide array of marketing activities.

When the regional offices received these campaigns, they were accompanied by the buyer persona that guided their development. During online meetings, the global team presented the buyer personas and asked the regional marketers to consider which of the insights, if any, might be different in their part of the world.

For instance, the global marketers asked their regional marketers in Latin America to review the Priority Initiative and Success Factor insights they had discovered, saying, "This is what we heard from

North American customers. Have you heard anything different about the buying triggers or key benefits of these solutions in Chile?"

If the regional marketers cited differences, the global marketers could discuss the specifics and assess the effect, if any, that those variables might have on any aspect of the campaign.

In some of the countries, the teams went on to talk to their salespeople or conduct surveys to validate the buyer persona insights in their location. Other marketers found the budget for interviews with their local buyers.

Although it is too soon to measure the effect of this program in terms of the original goal—delivering consistent campaigns and utilizing marketing budgets more effectively—the company has already seen changes in the conversation between the two parts of their organization. Rather than focusing on underutilized marketing assets, the teams are openly discussing the differences in their buyer personas and what they need to do to improve engagement.

Can You Be Useful to People Who Aren't Buying?

So far we've explored ways that you can rely on your buyer personas to market to people considering solutions like the one your organization offers. We urge you to address these opportunities first, as this is the shortest path to quality sales leads, revenue, and evidence that buyer personas work.

Ultimately, however, you will want your buyer personas to help you address a much more challenging long-term goal: engaging those people whose priorities lie elsewhere.

Yes, we know you have a solution that buyers want and that you can help them become more efficient, reduce stress, lower costs, or increase their business. Because many of these people have other initiatives that are consuming their time and resources, it isn't easy to get their attention or be helpful to them.

Marketing activities that address these buyers encompass thought leadership and inbound initiatives. Thought leadership is content that allows your buyer to see a problem or opportunity from an entirely new perspective, while inbound marketing is defined by content that is so useful that buyers will actively find it and want to learn more. Both of these ideas are commonly understood yet difficult to achieve.

Educate Buyers That Success Is within Reach

When attempting to engage or educate buyers who aren't actively considering your solution, you must first make them realize that your solution will address a problem that they have either overlooked or put aside while attending to bigger or more readily achievable issues.

Your Buying Insights contain two findings that will help you move this issue to the forefront of your buyer's attention. The Priority Initiative insight tells you how similar buyers became motivated to address the problem, and the Perceived Barriers insight reveals why buyers believe these solutions won't help them. Your strategy should convince buyers that they are being left behind as their peers make progress, and that your approach eliminates the obstacles to success.

Let's say that you have a Cloud solution for storing and analyzing huge data files, and your Priority Initiative insight tells you that Information Technology architects are moving their business intelligence solutions to the Cloud. The buyer persona's Perceived Barriers involve concerns about data privacy and security.

Now you need to resist the temptation to have someone inside your company prepare a white paper or lead an event that explains that your organization is solving these problems. Your Buyer's Journey insight tells you that buyers who aren't looking for a solution are the least likely to trust a resource prepared by a company that benefits from solving the problem. Instead, you will want to consult your buyer persona to understand which experts and resources your buyer trusts. These are the people you should contact to prepare the paper on your behalf. As part of your agreement with the authors, ensure that they will distribute the paper through their channels.

You can still circulate the paper through your own activities, of course, as this paper is equally likely to benefit the other buyers who are looking for your solution. But for buyers who aren't yet looking, make sure you have a soft call to action. Your relationship with this buyer is still very tenuous, so you need a series of useful assets that you can deliver without demanding the buyer's name and email address. If you turn the tables you will see that this buyer is not yet a lead. The buyer has only taken the first step to see if this topic should be a priority. One wrong step and the answer will be no, which is much easier to justify. You will need to invest wisely to ensure that you are delivering really useful information.

Here is one piece of specific advice for this delicate marketing activity. When we interview buyers about the resources they most value prior to their search, they tell us that they want original research and analysis. And they want it to be as brief and succinct as possible. In fact, one buyer recently told us that he would pay $1,000 for an opinion paper containing 100 pages, $2,000 for that same analysis in 10 pages, and if the information could be delivered in one page, it was worth $5,000 to him.

To initiate a relationship with buyers who aren't currently looking, be brief, be useful, and don't ask for anything in return.

Autodesk Helps Buyers Achieve Their Top Priorities

The final approach to reaching buyers who aren't yet looking at your solution involves identifying buyers' other priorities and providing guidance in those areas. The guiding principle here is that by demonstrating your commitment to your customers' success—particularly in an area unrelated to your primary focus—you will have established a foundation of trust that will facilitate future contact when they are in need of the product or service you are offering.

This can be the most difficult way to catch the attention of buyers because your content is likely to compete with other sources that are addressing the same topic. However, dramatic success is possible, as is demonstrated by the following story, a case study that should motivate every marketer who has ever had a vision for change but has been frustrated and unable to win influential support.

Autodesk is a prominent design software and services company that offers business solutions to many of the leading firms in the architecture, engineering, construction, manufacturing, media, and entertainment industries. An important segment of their business is working with very small businesses, companies ranging from 20 employees to some as small as one- or two-person shops.

When he became head of small-business marketing for Autodesk, Dusty DiMercurio discovered that few people in the company knew very much detail about this segment of their market. Autodesk's small-business customers were spread far and wide geographically and were relatively hard to find. It was even difficult to determine accurately how many there were. DiMercurio concluded that the best way to market to them was to get to know them better and try to understand their relationship with Autodesk and its products.

With a small-business marketing team, DiMercurio first contacted a number of his current customers and showed them Autodesk's existing marketing materials, their website, and other promotional tools, and listened to what they had to say.

The small-businesses owners responded that they were enthusiastic about Autodesk's products, but they found the website polished and slick. Many said, "It doesn't talk to me. I sense you guys are dealing with much larger, more sophisticated businesses. I'm just a little guy trying to run his own business."

Convinced that the company could do better, DiMercurio and his team conducted interviews with their potential buyers, including everyone from independent specialty contractors to architects who had left larger firms to start their own businesses.

It didn't take long for the Autodesk team to identify similarities, even though the interviews reflected a wide range of industries. "These daily business challenges can be demanding," many of the interviewees said. "I never went to business school. I never formally learned how to run a business."

As he was building his personas, DiMercurio found this insight especially revealing. "Thinking like a software vendor, you would assume their challenges would be related to becoming more productive with your product," DiMercurio recalled. "But those weren't their real challenges. Instead, we were hearing concerns such as, 'I don't know how to find customers. When I get customers, I don't know how to keep them coming back.' Their questions focused on a lot of operational things like, 'How do I best manage my business finances?'"

Already contemplating the creation of an inbound marketing program for their small-business customers, DiMercurio realized he needed to come up with unique Web content that would drive their buyers to find Autodesk and regularly return to hear what the company had to say. He knew his current website wasn't speaking to this persona.

"I realized that it would be really difficult to influence the Web team and ask them to change their existing design," DiMercurio said. "So I said to myself, 'I'll start a website with some really helpful content based on what I now know about our small-business customers' challenges.'" His interviews also revealed that his personas spent a lot of time on their mobile devices, so he knew he wanted to design the site for mobile use.

Autodesk already had procedures and guidelines around content creation, but DiMercurio decided not to follow most—if any—of them. "Almost everything we did was off brand," DiMercurio said. "However, we had good justification for it. We had talked to our customers and had data to prove that our engagement with them could be a lot more effective. In this way, I positioned our small-business marketing initiative internally as more of an incubator, a pilot."

DiMercurio had the opportunity to preview what he was working on with his senior vice president. He told his boss, "Most people hate being sold to. I want to create content that people love, a site that people actually want to follow. I want to turn traditional marketing on its head."

With Buying Insight from his persona interviews, DiMercurio continued gaining buy-in for his project. "We took a lot of risks, and internally, I kept the project under the radar for as long as I could," he says in retrospect. "I tried to keep it as stealth as possible until we had something to show for it. Luckily, I had air cover from my senior director at the time to do so."

DiMercurio didn't rely on many internal resources. He got the approval to add one content marketing manager and hired someone who had formerly been an editor of a national magazine. The two of them worked together to refine their small-business personas to understand precisely what content would engage them and then built an editorial strategy around that.

DiMercurio and his small team quietly built their alternative website with content geared toward helping small businesses be successful. They called it Line//Shape//Space with a subhead *Ideas and Inspiration for Your Business.* On it were pragmatic and practical articles covering basics such as "Five Trade Show Tips to Book a Booth and Not Lose Your Shirt" or "Four Questions to Ask before Starting a Company" to more specialized content like "Can Your Firm Afford to Offer a Proposal on a Federal Design and Build Contract?" and "Four Conversations Architects Must Have with Clients before Starting a Green Building Project." As a result of their buyer interviews, the team had discovered that the small businesses' challenges translated into roughly six content topics—money, learning, managing, stories, clients, and marketing—which, in turn, influenced the design of the website.

Following the guidelines for effective content marketing, promotion of Autodesk was kept to a minimum. When DiMercurio hired his content marketing manager, he intentionally sought out a professionally trained journalist rather than someone with a marketing background. DiMercurio believes that it's easier to train a journalist to become a good marketer than it is to train a marketer to become a good journalist. "In many ways, marketers are trained to talk about themselves," he says. "It's difficult to avoid that impulse." DiMercurio suggests that journalists are trained to do the opposite: to capture attention by discussing the topics that are most important to their audiences, all the while minimizing their own personal bias.

To help spread the word of his site among his target audience, DiMercurio partnered with Autodesk's industry marketing teams, many of whom were already developing campaigns targeting small businesses. He also used an assortment of diverse outbound tactics, from social media outreach to partnerships with other heavily trafficked industry blogs. He approached ArchDaily, a heavily visited architecture site, and offered them some practical small-business-related content in return for credit and a link that drove new traffic to Line//Shape//Space.

Some internal stakeholders expressed skepticism about Autodesk devoting creative time to a content marketing blog; however, marketers elsewhere in the company soon began approaching DiMercurio and his team with requests to reuse his content. He was happy for other departments to do so, but if an Autodesk marketer wanted to insert "sales-y" information about a particular product within the content, DiMercurio refused.

In retrospect, DiMercurio admits that a lot of his colleagues had to be educated about the most effective use of content marketing and the importance of editorial material that wasn't tied to an overt sales pitch. "I was fortunate to have had some senior executives here who understood what I was doing and protected my flank," he says. One senior executive advised his staff, "Your teams should be looking closely at the content on Line//Shape//Space."

The praise for DiMercurio and his small team didn't end there. In 2013 Line//Shape//Space was named an official honoree in the business blog category of the 18th Annual Webby Awards, alongside other highly esteemed journalistic publications such as TechCrunch, the *Atlantic,* and Mashable.

This was only the most notable in a growing list of citations. The site also garnered multiple awards from Content Marketing Institute, W3, Davey, and Communicator.

And what of Dusty DiMercurio?

Around the time of the awards, Autodesk senior executives inquired what direction he wanted to go next. "I told them, I would love to focus solely on content marketing, addressing a broader audience than just the small businesses," DiMercurio recalls. "I made the case that as modern marketing practices evolve, really cool storytelling has a great potential for engagement. And Autodesk has a really great story to tell. I put together my pitch and I presented it to them."

That became his new job. DiMercurio jumped up a couple of levels in the organization and was named head of content marketing, reporting to a VP of marketing. He was able to transition his whole small-business marketing team into a content marketing team devoted to creating editorial material for all of Autodesk's businesses, focusing on thought leadership, journalistic storytelling, and content that enables buyers and accelerates the sales pipeline.

And when asked for two lessons that other marketers might take away from his story, DiMercurio emphasized the critical value of Buyer Personas. "It's really important to understand who you're talking to; staying focused on what's really important to them should be your top priority."

After a pause, DiMercurio added, "And don't compromise."

Dusty DiMercurio's story is both wonderful yet highly unusual. Accomplishing something like this requires talent, timing, and executive support for a marketing investment that doesn't overtly communicate the value of your company's solutions.

Additionally, you will want to rigorously adhere to the rules for thought leadership and guidelines for inbound marketing. This involves building helpful information in areas outside of your company's core competency and working with experts in these topics. Many companies curate content from other sites, but far more power resides with a site that provides well-presented, valuable, original information. If you are providing precisely what buyers are looking for, they will seek it out and return again and again. Doing this successfully requires thinking like a publisher, creating content that keeps your target reader in mind, and being astutely aware of what they want to read.

Finally, don't even try to undertake this approach unless you work for a big company that has the tenacity to maintain this investment when someone questions the return on investment (ROI) or wonders if those funds couldn't be better invested in a lead generation activity. As the wise man said, "Don't compromise."

10 | Align Sales and Marketing to Help Buyers Decide

If you've worked in marketing for more than a decade, chances are you've received an all-too-common internal communication: an invitation to attend an "all-hands" meeting where senior management announces a reorganization of the marketing department. You may have experienced a sense of *déjà vu* as you heard that a new organizational structure is being implemented to "align our resources and greatly enhance our ability to achieve the company's critical goals and objectives."

Wait. Didn't you attend a meeting a few years ago announcing the reverse configuration? Or perhaps that one announced a different structural alignment, or even the decision to merge sales and marketing.

Plus ça change, plus c'est la même chose. Reorganizations are often prompted by shifts in upper-level management, challenging market conditions, or a recent acquisition. But no matter the triggering event, these structural shifts are merely symptomatic of a much bigger and more pervasive problem.

Quite simply, there is widespread concern about the lack of synergy between the marketing and sales organizations. A widely cited 2011 Forrester Research study revealed the sobering fact that 92 percent of business-to-business (B2B) companies report marketing and sales alignment problems. Undoubtedly, this situation is very bad for business, with buyers subjected to conflicting (or entirely irrelevant) strategies to win their business.

Companies have tried to solve this problem for as long as I've been in the industry. Among the most dramatic "solutions" is the one that reorganizes marketing to report directly to sales. On the surface, this is logical. If the purpose of marketing is to grow revenue and sales and marketing are not aligned, a single reporting structure would seem to address that problem.

From personal experience, I strongly believe that these approaches are not working and can even make it worse. Most of my career has been spent in marketing; I was a bag-carrying, commissioned sales rep for only a year. But I learned at least one lesson during the four years that I spent as senior vice president of sales and marketing: Marketing should not report to sales. The reason is simple. When marketing is managed by the executive who has to make this quarter's numbers, the marketing team's day-to-day priorities will naturally shift to those that are most likely to impact near-term results.

I've observed these reorganizations in countless companies over the last decade, but I'm not pointing fingers. I personally experienced this dilemma and responded the same way when I ran both sales and marketing. In a resource-constrained environment (is there another kind?) my daily decisions often prioritized short-term urgent activities at the expense of long-term strategic investments.

Our sales rep has a presentation that could produce a $300,000 deal this quarter? Pull a senior marketer off of that launch plan to make sure the rep is well prepared for the meeting. Under pressure to produce qualified leads? Who could blame marketing for insisting that even early stage buyers provide their name, email address, and more in exchange for the company's e-book? Is marketing's bonus tied to this quarter's revenue goal? It's easy to see why no one can find the time to interview buyers and build the strategies that will fill next year's pipeline.

Reorganizations won't solve anything; if there were magic in one of these formulas, we would have discovered it by now. This problem calls for an entirely new way of thinking. It's time to redefine marketing's relationship with sales, and the key to forging that partnership begins with a shared understanding of your buyers' expectations.

Changing the Conversation with Salespeople

Ask your most successful salespeople to describe their winning strategy, and they will undoubtedly talk about the trusted relationships they build with their customers. Sure, they need to understand your products, the competitive landscape, and how to deliver a compelling presentation. And yes, they want good leads and sales tools. But their core priority is to create strong customer partnerships. That's how they make quota, and for a sales rep, quota is everything.

With this simple explanation of the sales persona, think about your last meeting with that team. Did you talk about your upcoming promotional event, how many leads you hope to deliver, or maybe that product launch that's coming in the next few months? Were the salespeople listening to you, or were they preoccupied with their smartphones?

Imagine the change in that response if you started your next meeting by talking about the Buying Insights you've discovered through recent interviews. After all, in the course of your interviews you will have learned a great deal of information about the people they need to engage and will have details about what goes on behind the scenes that your buyers have never revealed to their salesperson.

Now you can tell your salespeople the good news: Our research confirms that these types of buyers want to meet with you, *and* not only do we know the reasons why, we know what they hope to hear from you as well. We know which types of buyers are in the buying center, what they object to, and what they are going to love.

This will get their attention. We promise. *Now* your reps are ready to hear about the marketing activities and sales tools you've created to help these buyers see the value of your approach.

Share Insights, Not Buyer Personas

One caveat, however. As with all communications, consider your audience. You want to provide information to salespeople in a format that they trust, will be receptive to, and can use. The buyer persona satisfies none of these criteria.

Because salespeople are correctly trained to view every customer as unique, they tend to be suspicious that it's possible to create an example buyer. Show up at a meeting with your buyer persona and the first slide they'll see is your Buyer Profile. Surprised by this unexpected contribution from marketing, they are likely to focus on one demographic detail and summarily discount all of the valuable findings you plan to deliver in the upcoming buying insight slides.

"Wait, I had lunch with that guy yesterday," a salesperson might say. "He's got that job, but he doesn't report to the CEO [chief executive officer]. He reports to the CTO [chief technology officer]. What else is wrong here?"

You might eventually be able to explain the methodology in this book, but we urge you to avoid this potential problem altogether and deliver your buyer persona insights in a format that's the most useful and easiest to digest.

We advise you to leave your Buyer Profile in the marketing department and help your salespeople understand your Buying Insights, which your salespeople will readily recognize as the intelligence that will help them anticipate their buyers' needs, concerns, and priorities. As you stand at the front of the room, you can say, "We've been interviewing people who have recently evaluated supply chain management solutions, including people who chose us and those who bought from the 'big time' competitor. Here's what we learned."

Deliver Buying Insights through Sales Playbooks

One of the most helpful ways to communicate Buying Insights to salespeople is by integrating them into existing sales tools such as sales playbooks or training courses. Salespeople don't need another resource to consult; instead, they should be able to access your buyer persona intelligence in a format they have come to rely upon and access regularly.

Because sales playbooks are typically organized around buying decisions or solutions, it should be relatively easy to see how you can update them to include the insights you collected through your interviews. For example, in the section defining all of the people involved in the buying decision: job titles, responsibilities, and experience, you may add any relevant information from your Buyer Profile. You may have to adjust the playbook template somewhat, but see if you can include information about the dynamics between these influencers, especially the way that each of these buyers impacts the buying decision—a Buyer's Journey insight.

Another section of the report should focus on the key points that a salesperson should communicate. This is the place to incorporate the work that you did in Chapter 8, where you identified the intersection between what your buyers want to hear and your strongest capabilities.

As most playbooks include a section on competitors, be sure to include your Perceived Barrier insights along with the message points that will help your salesperson overcome those objections and debunk the myths. You may also find some of these points in the Decision Criteria insight, especially if your buyers have expectations where there is a perceived gap or your approach is unexpected.

> Buyers of high-consideration solutions don't make decisions based on features or price. They choose the provider who is best able to earn their trust.

Enabling the Challenger Sale

Shortly after the global financial crisis of 2008, the Corporate Executive Board (CEB), a research and advisory services firm, sponsored a study looking into how businesses were coping with the economic downturn. After examining the performance of more than 3,000 salespeople at 90 B2B companies that were struggling with the weakened business environment, CEB's researchers discovered a fascinating fact: A small but productive group of sales representatives across a wide range of industries was consistently continuing to close deals with few adverse effects.

The CEB inquiry segmented the sales persona with five profiles that they labeled relationship builders, reactive problem solvers, hard workers, lone wolves, and challengers. It was the latter group, the challengers, who were thriving in the midst of the poor economy. In fact, the average results of this relatively small segment of salespeople comprised 200 percent of core sales performance, ranking far ahead of the other four personas.

When the book based on this study, *The Challenger Sale,* was released in 2011, sales executives took notice. The relationship-based sales model had undergone a radical transformation. It was no longer enough for salespeople to be helpful and responsive to their customers; salespeople needed to take control of the conversation. This rare breed of salespeople was equipped to be a forceful educator, teaching their customers about new ways to solve problems.

It goes without saying that challenger reps could be credible in this role only if they were extremely knowledgeable about their customers' priority initiatives and any perceived barriers to addressing them. Although we haven't spoken to any of the salespeople who participated in this study, it stands to reason that these challenger reps must have been very proactive, taking the initiative to understand their customers' business when no one expected that of them.

Now that the challenger sales approach has been enthusiastically promoted in sales training and elevated as the paradigm of choice for the next decade, many B2B sales executives are holding their salespeople to this new standard. This is an ideal opportunity for marketing to partner with sales to deliver the Buying Insights that will enable this difficult transition. When you are the source of deep insight into your buyers' goals and barriers, you can establish your status as a strategic resource to sales and can ensure that your messages, activities, and tools are designed to enable the challenger sale.

Helping Salespeople Break into the C-Suite

Salespeople are confronting yet another daunting change in their responsibilities as product line extensions, multiple acquisitions, and buying center dynamics require them to call on new types of buyers and, in some cases, their customers' most senior executives. For reps who thrive on their ability to build relationships, it is easy to see why someone who has been accustomed to meeting a midlevel technical buyer might be concerned about, for example, calling on the company's chief financial officer (CFO), who undoubtedly speaks a different language and will have questions that this rep has never had to answer before.

Although this is a dramatic example, this issue can be just as disruptive when an acquisition requires the salespeople to call on another type of midlevel manager about a completely different solution category.

Most companies are ill-equipped to address the core need in these circumstances—giving this sales team confidence that they have a persuasive story that will impress these new types of buyers and, quite frankly, that they won't look stupid. Imagine being the poor rep who, armed only with deep knowledge of the solution, finally gets a meeting with the CFO. If the rep talks about the product, the meeting is over. If the rep talks about the need to grow the business and increase profitability, the CFO will quickly observe that this conversation adds no value. Once again, the meeting is over and the salesperson is unlikely to have a second chance.

Marketers who have interviewed these buyers need to step into this situation with Buying Insights that explain the role that each of the influencers in the buying center plays during the search for a new solution, as well as their concerns and expectations. They can outline a typical buying scenario, describing the priority initiative that triggers the need for a solution, why each of the influencers became involved, and what they really care about.

This scenario should do more than convey the insights; it should also contain prescriptive suggestions. It might note, "At this point in the decision-making process, the CTO is primarily concerned with [one particular technical challenge] and does not want to be bothered hearing about the solution. He wants to hear about [specific answer] that is currently driving his need."

The narrative should outline the probable sequence of events, a rundown of the other buyers who will be involved, and the questions and answers that will be valuable to each of the buyers. For instance, there may be bulleted points that define exactly what the CFO wants to hear about; the role of the IT department and what they are looking for; which buyers are already favorably disposed toward your company and the reasons why; plus the reasons why some buyers may have negative perceptions about your company and how to counter them.

With your Buying Insights and the messaging work that you did in Chapter 8, you can provide the guidance your reps need to gain confidence in their ability to build these new relationships. For example:

- When meeting with the CTO, emphasize our ability to deliver consolidated reports across multiple databases. But expect the CTO to be concerned about the work that's needed to aggregate and normalize these databases and be prepared to talk about our services. You might want to bring a sales engineer along on this call. And here's a link to a white paper that explains our database integration methodology.

- The director of marketing hates presentations that walk through every aspect of the product. During the product demonstration, make sure to emphasize our dashboard and in particular, our ability to show the real-time trends around mobile purchases, because we know that this capability is among the director's top priorities and our trending is superior to any of the competitors. Go here for the demo instructions and a leave-behind that emphasizes the other capabilities he wants to hear about.

- When you receive a request for proposal (RFP) for this solution, check to see if these capabilities are among those that are requested, as this will tell you if Big Time competitor's salesperson was behind the creation of the RFP. If you want to win this deal, you will need to get a meeting with the head of supply chain management and focus on our ability to deliver these real-time reports (link) as he is our best advocate.

When you help your salespeople anticipate the conversation they will encounter with a new type of buyer, you are preparing them to succeed on more than the strength of your solution offering. Your reps know that trust, clarity, and authenticity are essential to success, and without this confidence, they will inevitably pursue the leads and contacts that are familiar to them and more likely to result in closed business.

Insight into the Nurse's Emotions Halts Sales Losses

When a leading manufacturer of complex medical equipment started losing market share, they suspected that a new dynamic among the influencers in their buying center was the source of the problem. But in this case study from Wayne Cerullo, managing partner of B2P Partners, we learn that the missing insight was about a buyer persona who had always been their target audience.

Illinois Scientific (IS), a pseudonym, is one of a handful of manufacturers of a medical monitoring device that is used around the clock for every patient in every hospital in the world. This device is so important and the consequences of error so grievous that before IS monitors are installed, nurses must undergo a lengthy implementation period that includes intensive technical training and hands-on experience.

When a single hospital purchases these monitors, each sale is worth millions of dollars to the winning supplier—and a huge commission for the sales team. IS had long been a market leader in this category based on its reputation for devices with superior reliability. In sales presentations, the account managers knew that they needed to emphasize the way the IS monitors were designed to avoid unnecessary complexity and convey vital information in a clear display. They noted specific safeguards and accommodations that made it harder to press the wrong button or enter erroneous data that could have fatal repercussions.

Despite the fact that the product quality was as strong as ever, a relative newcomer had begun to erode IS's market position, triggering a gradual decline that was perplexing to the sales team and beginning to affect the bottom line. The team was hearing that IS was no longer perceived to be a leading-edge supplier, but it was unclear what they needed to do about it.

Suspecting that a buying center dynamic was involved, IS invested in interviews with their traditional buyer, the head of the nursing department, plus buying influencers from pharmacology, electronic health records (EHR) experts, patient safety officers (PSO), and biomedical technical specialists, the health care technology engineers who make sure the equipment is checked and running properly.

While their interviews identified the contrasting concerns and perspectives of these five different personas, IS's interviews with the nursing staff were the most revealing. In every conversation, they listened as nurses described the overworked, underpaid, overstressed, and underappreciated aspects of their positions. While overseeing the lives of hundreds of people every day, they could seldom escape their human fallibility. Many were haunted by the memory of moments they nearly came to regret, such as almost failing to see a badly printed decimal point during a long night working in an intensive care unit (ICU)—a scenario in which the difference between 0.5 percent ml and 5 percent ml was a life or death mistake.

IS was aware of the risks and had designed their products to help. Salespeople knew to emphasize these features in their sales presentations. But until the IS team conducted their interviews, they didn't realize the extent to which these daily stresses permeated the nurses' working environment—and more critically, how it affected their preference for the competitor's monitoring devices.

Although IS products were top of the line and the training and technical support were regarded as superb, it was apparent in buyer interviews that IS wasn't paying sufficient attention to the intensive emotional culture. And they had no idea that their comparatively smaller competition was beating them with that specific strategy.

The team learned that their account team's explanation of the device's specifications was failing to move the audience by missing the larger context in which the mechanism was being used. Removed from the emotional realities of a daily hospital environment, an emphasis on technical features—such as "speeds and feeds"—could sound absurdly incongruous. (One can easily imagine a health worker whispering to another, "And what planet is he from?") Within the larger medical community this was slowly beginning to define IS and its reputation.

In contrast, IS's interviews revealed that its smaller competitor was going out of its way to include small, but significantly meaningful gestures of appreciation and empathy to members of the hospital team. In one interview, the nurses recalled that their competitor's technical aide stayed up all night to help the overnight nursing team during the initial implementation. The next time the aide visited the hospital, she brought doughnuts.

When hospitals were shopping for new monitoring equipment, they contacted peer medical facilities to ask for recommendations. The "doughnut" story was often retold and passed along to other prospective buyers.

Realizing that they were missing the human side of the buying decision, IS instituted a new sales and service strategy that emphasized these "Five Cs of Excellence":

- *Composition* of the team: Match members of the IS team with each buyer persona's specialties and make sure they understand that persona's goals, needs, and concerns. Now IS biomed specialists are assigned to work directly with the hospital's biomed people; IS patient safety specialists will work with the PSOs, and so on.
- *Communication*: Members of the IS implementation team were trained to listen and watch for hospital workers' reactions as they presented and installed the IS devices. The IS team learned how to respond effectively to their customers' concerns, even if they were unfounded.
- *Commitment*: This was a reminder to the team to consistently demonstrate a commitment to helping the hospital deliver the most effective health care. For the salespeople, this included a clear message that they needed to watch for any communication that might sound like they were looking for more business. Instead, the team was instructed to go the extra mile to ensure a successful implementation, even if it extends the job beyond the planned time frame.
- *Connection*: Acknowledge that health care workers are people who intrinsically care about others. Speak their language by demonstrating mutual understanding; understand the importance of eye contact, cordiality, warmth, and empathy.
- un*Common* acts: Never underestimate the power of the unexpected gesture or action that demonstrates caring and appreciation. These are what are often talked about years later.

Focusing on these five points, IS radically reorganized how the sales and service teams were organized and trained. Knowledgeable specialists were matched with their hospital counterparts, and new emphasis was placed on hiring team members who had excellent people and communication skills.

In place of technical presentations featuring the buttons and controls on their monitors, the sales team engaged their listeners with a dramatic story showing how IS was working with these five core principles. IS framed its story by calling attention to an unsung hero: the overworked, underpaid, and overstressed hospital health care worker.

Integrated messaging in sales presentations, promotional campaigns, and white papers reinforced IS's commitment to reducing their customers' daily stresses; everything from carefully designing their medical equipment with clearly discernable audible, visual, and tactile safeguards to facilitating better interaction between the nursing staff and other members of the medical community.

Not only did IS openly acknowledge the realities of the daily hospital subculture, it did so by demonstrating that it understood the importance of listening and responding to its clients, core values that health care workers themselves believe should define their choice of vocation.

For marketing, this new strategy significantly redefined their relationship with the IS salespeople. The new implementation campaign and the supporting story gave sales the tools it needed to reverse the eroding market. And as a result marketing was now recognized by IS sales as a valued partner—a nontrivial outcome!

Sales and Marketing: Vive La Différence!

In 2011, the century-old Chartered Institute of Marketing (CIM), which describes itself as "the world's largest organization for

professional marketers," went so far as to release a paper recommending the fusion of sales and marketing during the coming decade. Their
proposal: Bury the hatchet, admit *mea culpa,* and make marketing
report directly to sales.

This is no vision for the future. What if understanding and
addressing your buyer's expectations—working together to tell a story
that builds trust between your company and your customer—became
the new common ground to align sales and marketing?

Cancel the meetings where marketing updates salespeople about
the latest promotional campaigns, the ongoing initiatives for lead
generation, or the success of the latest product launch. You can
communicate those updates via email or a marketing newsletter.

When marketing and sales get together, use the time for a
conversation in which salespeople can report what they are hearing
from buyers and compare their reports with what marketing is
learning from buyer interviews. When every conversation between
sales and marketing centers on what buyers want, and when marketing
provides demonstrated expert knowledge about buyer insight, the
teams will naturally align to respond to their customer's expectations.

Salespeople aren't paid to look for patterns and trends. That's
marketing's specialty. Salespeople are paid to treat every account as
unique, and that's what they should do. There's no reason to turn
salespeople into marketing people. And conversely, there's no reason
to turn marketing people into salespeople. Both provide invaluable
and necessary roles. There is a need for some people to focus on
the horizon and work to create a reputation that will generate future
opportunities. And there is a need for others to make sure that cash is
coming in the door during next quarter.

By confirming that sales and marketing have the same goals but
distinctly different competencies and timelines, we can move ahead
and meet on common ground: aligning our story with the one our
buyers want to hear.

11 | Start Small, with an Eye to the Future

Knowledge is power.

These three words appear in quotations that have been cited and repeated countless times. An Internet search attributes this phrase to a wide variety of familiar names ranging from Sir Francis Bacon and Kofi Anan to Tom Clancy and Mary J. Blige.

Perhaps a cliché, and yet, as with most clichés, within it resides the truth.

It's a theme that appears in numerous episodes of the original *Star Trek* series, in stories about people who become powerful after acquiring new knowledge. The inhabitants of a troubled planet who followed the instructions of an idol or disembodied brains learn that their leadership is merely an illusion, a machine, or a supremely fallible mortal. Once the truth is revealed to the citizens of the planet, our heroes, Captain Kirk and his crew, warp away on the *Enterprise,* leaving the inhabitants to take control of their lives.

We can't promise that the knowledge and insights that you will gain by interviewing your buyers will make you a hero, but we do

185

know that you will have the power to quickly effect dramatic change in your company and take more control over the strategies we've discussed.

The logic is inescapable. Your buyer interviews will give you insight into the factors that influence buyers' decisions. With this clearly defined information, you can become a trusted authoritative resource within your company: the one person to consult for guidance on messaging and activities intended to convince buyers to choose your organization's solution. As the source of Buying Insight, you will possess the knowledge your salespeople need to align the strategies intended to win your buyer's business.

You may choose to stop there. But before we end, we want to reveal just a bit more about potential ways to leverage buyer personas.

Where to Begin Your Buyer Persona Initiative

Over the years I've presented the concepts in this book to experienced marketers at countless seminars and workshops. When they realize they can use buyer personas to focus their strategies and achieve their goals, the energy and sense of excitement in the room is almost palpable.

Yet I'll never forget the marketer who approached me at the end of the session: "Wow! This is the most amazing idea I've ever heard. It's so logical. And it has the power to change my life."

And then he changed the tone of his voice. "The only problem is that you are assuming our management is logical."

Persuading key stakeholders—either the decision makers within your organization or a client of your marketing agency—can be a difficult. Stakeholders who express reluctance to engage in buyer persona research sometimes worry that if they go down this path they may need to build personas for every product in their company.

Contrasting this resistance, there are the extremely excited visionaries who begin imagining all the potential possibilities. Marketers at large companies tell me, "We really want to do this! I want to build personas across all of our solutions, for every decision buyers make, for every buyer we know." As excited as we are too, we strongly urge you not to undertake anything like this. Not yet anyway.

Recall our advice from Chapter 4—you will want to start with one well-defined project, goal, or campaign of strategic interest to your stakeholders. It should be one that everyone agrees cannot be achieved by doing business as usual. With the outcome defined as something your stakeholders acknowledge will be difficult, you will have established the grounds to test the value of your buyer persona initiative. And once you can point to proven results, you will have earned support for using buyer personas to make future decisions about the messaging and activities that engage buyers to choose you.

Choosing the right place to begin may seem a bit daunting, but the selection of a challenging goal will make it more difficult for anyone to claim after the fact that your results could have been obtained without your buyer persona.

For example, your organization may be entering markets that require your salespeople to call on an entirely new type of buyer. Or you may want to market a solution that combines an existing product with one that was acquired through a merger. Or perhaps your company is suddenly experiencing competitive pressure in a market where you had previously been the acknowledged leader.

If your company has been struggling with these problems, it is highly likely that the insight from this single project will be met with surprise . . . possibly astonishment. Where previously the path to success was unknown, your stakeholders will now understand the Priority Initiative that causes buyers to take action, the Success Factors that motivate them, and the Perceived Barriers that have been thwarting your efforts. Rather than a mass or scattershot campaign, the Buyer's Journey will show them which buyers are most critical to reach, and through your Decision Criteria insights, they'll know whether your solution and company have what it takes to win this business.

You want a dramatic demonstration that shows that a small, focused buyer persona initiative can make a lasting impression. Only after this impression has been made dramatically and forcefully—and won over allies and convinced influential stakeholders—should you begin to build buyer personas for other parts of your business.

Don't be concerned about going slowly. We know of no companies that have fully integrated buyer personas into all of the activities detailed in the pages of this book. As of this writing, even the major corporations that are using this methodology have focused only on selected marketing initiatives.

How to Earn Your Stripes as a Strategic Resource

It is our vision that once stakeholders begin to trust buyer personas to guide their decisions, they will start thinking of marketers as the buyer experts, authorities who can be counted upon to guide the company's strategies to reach new markets, achieve difficult goals, or overcome competitive obstacles.

I've always noticed that no one questions the assumption that the finance team is best qualified to keep the books or that engineering is most knowledgeable about building useful products. But marketing tends to be everyone's playground.

One reason for this contrasting perception of disciplines is the fact that unlike other professional roles, marketers have not been positioned as the owners of specialized, high-value competencies. Senior management entrusts the IT department with complex decisions because they have extensive knowledge of available technologies and how they can be applied to the company's business.

Once marketers are perceived as buyer experts, they should be given similar authority to affect decisions that impact buyers and customers. From acquisitions to market expansion and product extensions, the buyer's perspective is of utmost importance to the success or failure of these initiatives. There is currently a vacuum of Buying Insight inside most corporations. Marketers need to own that competency.

I have no illusions that this transformation will occur swiftly and suddenly. But small changes can make a big difference. Consider the way many marketers speak in meetings. It's common for marketers to preface their remarks with phrases such as, "I think," or "From where I sit, it seems to me that . . ." Instead, marketers should strive to remove the first-person pronouns and channel the authority of the buyer's voice.

At any meeting where your buyers' opinion is relevant, make an effort to start your sentence with, "We've been listening to buyers and here's what they think," or "We have been interviewing buyers, and they said they wanted . . ."

As a proxy for your buyer, you should have the confidence to speak with authority and bring your buyer's voice to that decision. Making statements such as these may raise questions about how recently you have spoken to these buyers, so be prepared to back up your comments. If you are conducting your own interviews, we generally recommend that you conduct one interview a month, because this makes it easy to provide the answer everyone wants to hear.

In reality, however, it may surprise you that Buying Insights do not change as often as you think, and when they do, you will likely be aware that you need to engage in additional interviews. That's because the primary triggers for these changes are big news—a major upturn or downturn in economic conditions, the merger or divestiture initiated by a significant competitor, or a new government regulation that requires your customers to make an investment in a solution like the one your organization offers. Major advances in technology or security problems are other factors that affect Buying Insights, but once again, these will be highly obvious to you and everyone else. If any of these occur, and depending on the severity of the change, you will want to invest in another round of interviews to understand how your buyer's mind-set may have shifted.

If you use a third party to conduct your buyer interviews and if no significant changes have occurred, you might consider asking your vendor to conduct a few new interviews once every six months or year. It is highly unlikely that the changes will be substantive, but this should handle the perception that your insights are not current enough to rely upon.

How Buyer Personas Benefit Product Strategy

As we discussed in Chapter 2, when Alan Cooper first pioneered the use of personas his mental exercise concentrated on the mind-set of the end user. His breakthrough led to the widespread practice of building user personas to guide the development of user-friendly software (for which we are eternally grateful).

However, the application of buyer personas for product strategy is far less common, and the consequences can be expensive. You may recall our story told in Chapter 1 about a technology firm that developed an innovative software product designed to assist processing maritime law. The product was almost ready to launch by the time the buyer interviews revealed that the market for the product was nonexistent. This insight saved the company from the expense and embarrassment of a failed launch, but it could have saved much more had they conducted this research a year before assigning their developers to build a product that would never be released.

Donato Mangialardo encountered a similar problem that had a very different outcome when, as a senior product manager for Balok Solutions (a pseudonym), he was asked to oversee a new Cloud solution for product lifecycle management (PLM). This is the software that is used in large enterprise manufacturing companies to manage every step of their process, from product design through materials acquisition and production.

Balok Solutions had engineered an important and innovative new feature into their solution enabling the software that was used to design new products to integrate with the PLM software. This innovation would help their client manufacturers avoid costly mistakes such as using the wrong supplier or part, or prevent costly and potentially dangerous mistakes that could result in a product recall.

This new feature appeared to be a fantastic addition, but Balok Solutions had not yet closed one sale of the new solution.

Mangialardo knew that he needed answers to four questions:

1. Which of the many roles in the manufacturer's organization is most concerned about this problem?
2. How prevalent is this problem and what is the buyer's perception about the cause?
3. What do buyers perceive as the consequences of the problem?
4. Who is the economic buyer who controls the budget for this purchase?

When Mangialardo realized that no one inside the company had asked these questions, he started interviewing buyers to get the answers. When he related this story to me, Mangialardo reflected on his Aha experience, "The moment when the persona crystallizes in your mind is just unforgettable. . . . I had nailed it."

His insight was so essential to the team's subsequent success that I'm not permitted to share it with you. But by creating a user persona for the engineering user and a buyer persona for the vice president of operations, Mangialardo was able to guide the development effort and shape a marketing strategy that earned him accolades throughout the company. The solution was central to the company's success over the coming years and Mangialardo was promoted to director of product management. Now, five years after this story, Mangialardo has leveraged the skills he perfected while at Balok Solutions to become vice president of marketing for a new company.

Building Buyer Personas for New Products

Donato Mangialardo's story gives us a glimpse of the value of having a product manager who knows that it's essential to impress both user and buyer personas. However, if you are not in product management and have earned a reputation as your company's buyer expert, you may be the one who is asked to initiate interviews that will guide new product decisions.

These interviews involve a slightly modified approach to the interviews we described in Chapter 5. In this case you will not have existing lists of the buyers to interview, so you will need to employ the services of a professional recruiter who sources participants for qualified interviews. (Professional recruiters are discussed in Chapter 4.)

As you think about whom you will interview, remember that your new product will compete against any other solution your buyers can use to solve the same problem. Your goal is to interview recent buyers of those solutions.

Let's consider the development of the iWatch, which combines many of the features of the contemporary smartphone with the miniaturization and portability of the wristwatch. Clearly, insight into the mind-set and expectations of heavy users of smartphones would be very helpful. We would want to hear the thoughts of people who we imagine would be early adopters of our device—those who are so attached to their smartphones that they already think of it as an extension of their body. These are clearly not among the many cell phone users who place their device in a handbag or regularly leave it in another room.

The interviews should begin with the opening question asking buyers to think back to the day when they first decided to evaluate a solution in this category. You will still want to listen carefully and ask probing questions to discover the 5 Rings of Buying Insight. However, toward the end of the interview you will introduce a question that reflects the company's vision for your new product.

This is the way the question should be posed: "We are talking to other [buyer role], and they tell us that if that if they had [new capability] it would [anticipated benefit]. What are your thoughts?" Here is the example: "We are talking to other heavy users of smartphones who tell us that if they could read and respond to their text messages on their watch, it would help them to respond faster and stay closer to their friends. What are your thoughts?"

You can ask more than one of these questions in a single interview: "These users also tell us that if the new watch included a mobile payment capability they would use it for every purchase they made. What are your thoughts?"

It's important to ask these questions at the end of the interview, after you've heard your buyers' stories about a recent evaluation of the solution you will be competing against. In this context, you will note any change in their emotional response and they may naturally tell you how they expect that this capability would have factored into their decision.

When you are having this conversation, be careful to avoid any attempt to persuade the buyer about the value of your solution. This is not a sales call, and you don't want to bias the responses. Stay neutral, emphasize that other buyers are telling you this, and record what the buyer has to say.

Communicating Insights That Affect Other Teams

As you listen to your buyers describe their experience evaluating your existing solutions, you are likely to learn about non-marketing-related matters that are affecting your ability to win their business.

These opportunities are most likely to show up as part of your buyers' Decision Criteria or Perceived Barriers, revealing that your company is not meeting your buyers' expectations in the area of sales, service, or product functionality. It could be that your product doesn't effectively integrate with a particular network or infrastructure. Maybe it doesn't create the kind of reports that are in demand. Or perhaps you discover something similar to Illinois Scientific, that is, that your reputation for sales and implementation services is having an unfavorable impact on your buyers' decisions.

We advise you to be cautious when you make any of these discoveries, especially if this is your first buyer persona and you are still working to gain the confidence of your internal stakeholders. Remember that your primary goal is to gain guidance for changes that will improve your marketing activities.

For example, if you hear that your buyers consistently have the same incorrect perception about your solution, avoid the impulse to complain to sales that they are failing to communicate correctly with potential buyers. Instead, your first step is to own the problem and invest in marketing activities intended to debunk the misperception. If this is one of your buyer's critical expectations, make it one of the key messages on your website or create an e-book about your approach. Reinforce the need for sales to emphasize that capability in your sales training or playbooks.

Once you've taken these steps and won your stakeholders' support for the value that buyer personas deliver to marketing, you may want to take your product-related findings to your development team. If there are sales-related problems, we urge you to take that finding to a senior manager in marketing and ask them to facilitate the communication to sales management. This will be a sensitive conversation, and you don't want to do anything that might interfere with your ability to continue to conduct these valuable interviews.

Using Buyer Personas to Guide Strategic Planning

Let's look into the future and consider marketing's new role in strategic planning once buyer personas have become an accepted part of your company's marketing activities and your marketing team is positioned as the company's respected buyer experts.

Whenever I talk to the technology industry, I can't address the subject of strategic planning without the name Steve Jobs being raised during the conversation. Jobs, who was legendary for his visionary foresight, was also well known for rejecting the value of market research. But one of the reasons Steve Jobs is legendary is that he was unique. He possessed an exceptional, perhaps genius ability to perceive market problems and needs and use this knowledge to drive the strategic direction of his company.

On occasions when people ask me about Jobs's attitude toward market research, this is my honest response: If you've got a Steve Jobs in your company, don't listen to me a minute longer. Go sit at his feet, listen to what he has to say, and do whatever he tells you. But if you're working with mere mortals in a typical company, you'll want to have a methodology that produces the insight you need to make buyer-focused decisions.

Of the countless decisions that your company makes, among the most challenging are the choices in the strategic plan. This is where your senior-level executives make commitments of resources and budget by evaluating their opportunities for growth in the coming years.

At the table are members of the C-suite offices, including the chief marketing officer (CMO), who is expected, among other topics, to recommend a marketing budget that will support the company's projected revenue growth. Most often, these decisions are guided by historical patterns of investments and returns. If there is any "market data" in the room, it is likely based on analyst predictions about the growth in your core markets.

Now the company must use these data to project its revenue, and in large companies, to determine which of its solutions will get the most development, sales and marketing investment. As many companies determine the marketing budget as a percentage of revenue, you can imagine the tension in the room. The CMO wants the right budget, but no one wants to forecast a revenue number that the team cannot achieve.

We envision a future where another source will add significant intelligence to this decision. At this point you will have buyer personas for most of your current products plus those that will launch during the coming year. For the first time, your CMO can design and defend marketing plans based on what buyers are saying about the resources they need and the places they expect to find them. The investment in marketing to a new audience can be justified with insight about that buying influencer's role to initiate the purchase or choose the provider. He or she can even defend the decision to invest far less than, or far more than, the industry average for marketing expenses as a share of revenue, because with this clear case to invest, it becomes a strategy that will win more business.

In our vision, you will have included the question from Chapter 5 about your buyer's top priorities for the coming year, so your CMO can also guide decisions about which products need the most invest-ment, saying: "Let's not put our bets on product A next year, because it's really product C that buyers say is their priority."

Perhaps you will have also invested in another interviewing technique that provides more visionary insight into the long-range priorities for specific buyers. In contrast to the interviews with buyers about recent decisions, these interviews focus on larger trends and conceptual issues in the marketplace. It's an advanced skill that calls for the experience of a professional interviewer, or someone who already has become comfortably adept at conducting probing inquiries. These interviews would help your CMO to identify buyer needs years in advance, with questions such as:

- How will the use of Big Data change the way business is done?
- What is next with the Cloud?
- Where is the idea of driverless cars going?
- What is the next evolution in green housing?

Unlike the buyer stories featured throughout this book, these interviews require you to introduce a topic that the buyer may or may not have contemplated. It is extremely easy to bias the outcome of these interviews and, as a result, collect data that are unreliable. So, with a recommendation that such exchanges are best conducted by an experienced interviewer, here, nevertheless, is the concept.

The first question should be defined around an issue or priority that your company hopes will be relevant in the coming years. For instance, your opening question might be, "We've been interviewing a number of retailers about drone delivery services, and one of the things we're hearing is their concern about the drone's limited battery life. We are hearing deep concern that gas-powered engines appear to be the far more practical option. What are your thoughts about that?"

Alternatively, you might want to explore the financial considerations of this solution, asking a different question, "We've been talking to other retailers about delivery drones, and we're hearing that this is going to allow them to deliver more items while cutting both their manpower and delivery time. They report they are now starting to make huge investments in this technology and are rushing to be among the first to offer this service. What are you thoughts about that?"

The model for beginning this kind of interview is, "We've been talking to other people like you and one of the things we're hearing . . ." and then you insert a trend or issue that you see developing in the market that your company wants to capitalize on, followed by a conclusion that's somewhat provocative.

The reason we want to make it provocative is that we want to elicit an emotional reaction from the buyer. Some will respond, "No way! Those batteries last only 10 minutes, and that isn't going to help me, except in very dense markets. I would love to use a gasoline-powered engine, but my customers aren't going to want a noisy weed-whacker flying over their heads." Or, "This is a Buck Rogers fantasy. We're not going to invest in this." Or you might get the buyer who says, "Absolutely, we agree completely. Gas-powered engines are the only way delivery drones are going to happen, and here's why . . ."

With these reactions you can begin to get a sense of buyers' current attitudes around a solution that your company sees as a part of your long-term strategy. It's a completely different method of conducting buyer interviews, and we caution you not to start here, but in combination with the fundamental interviewing covered throughout the book, we predict a future where your CMO will have increasingly valuable input to your company's most strategic decisions.

Start Small and Make a Big Difference

No one we know is using buyer personas in all these ways. Keep these more advanced ideas filed away until you are in a position to use them.

Despite all the exciting things you may want to accomplish, we urge you—in fact, we *plead* with you—go slowly and start with one critical project. You will never have the opportunity to explore any of these possibilities unless you can establish the credibility, authority, and influence of buyer personas with your first project. We remind you to choose one focused yet difficult project, goal, or campaign that is acknowledged to be of strategic importance to all stakeholders—and make a big statement about the value of buyer personas.

Buyer personas are an incredibly powerful tool when used correctly. We know from working with thousands of business professionals that the methodology detailed in this book can achieve all the things we've described in the first 10 chapters of this book. In this last chapter we have given you a glimpse of the impressive future that you might experience as you master these skills.

We are excited about the extended potential for buyer personas and privileged to travel this path with the world's most amazing marketers. We can't wait to see where this takes all of us.

For now, start small and make a big difference.

Bibliography

Angwin, Julia. "Why Online Tracking Is Getting Creepier," *ProPublica*, June 12, 2014. http://www.propublica.org/article/why-online-tracking-is-getting-creepier.

Argus Labs. "Finishing Up Its US $1.5M Seed Round, Argus Labs Seeks to Expand Its Team and Rolls Out Precision Targeting Technology," April 27, 2014. http://press.sentiance.com/71845-finishing-up-its-us-1-5m-seed-round-argus-labs-seeks-to-expand-its-team-and-rolls-out-precision-targeting-technology.

Baer, Jay. *Youtility: Why Smart Marketing Is About Help Not Hype*. New York, NY: Portfolio/Penguin, 2013.

Berkowitz, Joe. "The Art of the Interview: Dick Cavett on How to Elevate a Q&A," *Fastcocreate.com*, December 4, 2012. http://www.fastcocreate.com/1682030/the-art-of-the-interview-dick-cavett-on-how-to-elevate-a-qa.

Chartered Institute of Marketing. "Marketing and Sales Fusion," Cookham, Berkshire: Chartered Institute of Marketing, 2011. http://www.cim.co.uk/files/msfusion.pdf.

Chen, Brian X. "Why the Japanese Hate the iPhone," *Wired.com*, February 26, 2009. http://www.wired.com/2009/02/why-the-iphone.

Chen, Brian X. "Free, Video-Enabled iPhone 3GS Charms Japanese Consumers," *Wired.com*, August 18, 2009. http://www.wired.com/2009/08/iphone-japan.

Cooper, Alan. *The Inmates Are Running the Asylum: Why High-Tech Products Drive Us Crazy and How to Restore the Sanity*. Indianapolis, IN: Sams, 1999.

Cooper, Alan. "The Origins of Personas," *Cooper Journal*, May 15, 2008. http://www.cooper.com/journal/2008/05/the_origin_of_personas.

Corporate Executive Board's Marketing Leadership Council. "The Digital Evolution in B2B Marketing," Corporate Executive Board's Marketing Leadership Council, 2012. http://www .executiveboard.com/exbd-resources/content/digital-evolution/pdf/Digital-Evolution-in-B2B-Marketing.pdf.

Dixon, Matthew, and Brent Adamson. *The Challenger Sale: Taking Control of the Customer Conversation*. New York, NY: Portfolio/Penguin, 2011.

Eisenberg, Jeffrey, Bryan Eisenberg, and Anthony Garcia. *Buyer Legends: The Executive Storyteller's Guide*. Cardiff, CA: Waterfront Digital Press, 2014, e-book edition.

"Forrester Finds Most B-to-B Organizations Not Aligned," *Advertising Age*, January 28, 2011. http://adage.com/article/btob/forrester-finds-b-b-organizations-aligned/283186/?btob=1.

Geneen, Harold T., and Alvin Moscow. *Managing*. New York, NY: Doubleday, 1984.

Gilpin, Kenneth N. "Harold S. Geneen, 87, Dies; Nurtured ITT," *New York Times*, November 23, 1997.

Handley, Ann. *Everyone Writes: Your Go-To Guide to Creating Ridiculously Good Content*. Hoboken, NJ: John Wiley & Sons, 2014.

Jones, Chuck. "Apple's iPhone Captured 34% of Japanese Mobile Phone Sales in September," *Forbes.com*, October 28, 2013. http://www.forbes.com/sites/chuckjones/2013/10/28/apples-iphone-captured-34-of-japanese-mobile-phone-sales-in-september.

Lillian, Jessica. "Summit 2013 Highlights: Inciting a B-to-B Content Revolution," *Siriusdecisions.com*, May 9, 2013. https://www

.siriusdecisions.com/Blog/2013/May/Summit-2013-Highlights-Inciting-a-BtoB-Content-Revolution.aspx.

McKenna, Regis. *The Regis Touch: Million-Dollar Advice from America's Top Marketing Consultant.* Reading, MA: Addison-Wesley, 1985.

Sager, Ira, Peter Burrows, and Andy Reinhardt."Back to the Future at Apple," *Businessweek*, May 24, 1998.

Scott, David Meerman. "How Beko Develops Products Global Consumers Are Eager to Buy," *WebInkNow.com*, June 16, 2014. http://www.webinknow.com/2014/06/how-beko-develops-products-global-consumers-are-eager-to-buy.html.

Schwabel, Dan. "Stephen R. Covey Revisits the 7 Habits of Highly Effective People," *Forbes.com,* September 1, 2011. http://www.forbes.com/sites/danschawbel/2011/09/01/stephen-r-covey-revisits-the-habits-of-highly-effective-people/2.

Stone, Linda. "Continuous Partial Attention—Not the Same as Multi-Tasking," *Businessweek.com,* July 24, 2008. http://www.businessweek.com/business_at_work/time_management/archives/2008/07/continuous_part.html

Wood, Tom. "Three Old Chestnuts Cracked," *Foolproof*, April 6, 2011. http://www.foolproof.co.uk/thinking/three-old-chestnuts-cracked.

Index

Note: Page references in *italics* refer to figures and tables.

A

Aberdeen Group, 31

alignment, 131–164

  with Buyer's Journey (*See* Buyer's Journey)

  with salespeople (*See* sales department)

  with product strategy, 190–191

analysis of buyer interviews (*See* interview analysis)

Apple

  iPhone, 3–4, 5–6, 160

  iWatch, 192–193

  Jobs and, 4, 195

  Macintosh, 22

ArchDaily, 168

Archimedes, 19

Argus Labs, 46

audio recording, of interview, 77–78

Autodesk, 164–170

Acxiom, 46

B

Baer, Jay, 151, 152

Beko, 6–7

big data, 45–48

Brenner, Michael, 50

business-to-business (B2B)

  Buyer Persona approach for, xxii

  Buyer Profiles and social media, 49, 129

  identifying interviewees for, 64

  sales organization's contribution to insights, 42–43

business-to-consumer (B2C)

  Buyer Persona approach for, xxii

  identifying interviewees for, 64

Businessweek, 4

*Buyer Legends: The Executive
Storyteller's Guide*
(Eisenberg, Eisenberg),
41–42

Buyer Personas
building the presentation,
123–128, *124, 125, 126,
127*
C-level executive (case study),
31–34
completion time for, 52
defined, xx–xxii
early conception of, 20–23
expectations of buyers and,
23–25
5 Rings of Buying Insight for,
25–31 (*See also* 5 Rings of
Buying Insight)
to guide strategic planning,
194–198
"high-detail persona," 159
industry marketing affected
by, 158–160
inspiration from insight and,
19–20
product strategy benefits,
190–191, 192–193
"results-oriented persona,"
159–160
two *versus* one, 118–123, *119,
120, 121* (*See also*
segmentation)

vision for, 185–186, 188–190,
194–198
(*See also* goal setting; interview
analysis; interviewee
recruiting; interviews;
interview techniques)

Buyer Profiles
building, 129–130
Buyer Personas compared to,
7–10, *8*, 11–12
Buying Insight *versus*, 112–114
social media for, 48–49, 130

Buyer's Expectations
goal setting and, 184
interview analysis and, 106
messaging strategy and, 140–
141, 142, 143
revealing, xx, xxi
See also Buying Insight; 5
Rings of Buying Insight

Buyer's Journey (Buying Insight
4), 135–150, 151–170
alignment (*See* goal setting;
messaging strategy; sales
departments)
Autodesk example, 164–170
Caterpillar example, 159–160
crafting a buyer's story with,
41–42
defined, 26–27
educating buyers and, 163–164
example of, *127*, 154–155,
156

expectations for, 157–158

global perspective on, 160–162

goal setting and, 187

interview analysis for, 99–110

for long-term goals, 162–163

"Patrick" case study, 154–158

prioritizing assets for solution marketing, 156–157

Priority Initiative of buyers and, 151–152

understanding, 153–154

Web analytics and, 49–50, 158

(*See also* Buying Insights, decision making by buyers, interviews, interviewing techniques)

Buying Insight, 19–34

copywriting, 127–128

inspiration and insight, 19–20

interview analysis and "Insights Aggregator," 103–105, *104, 105*

interview analysis for Key Insights, 106–110, *107, 108, 109,* 117

interviewing for, 73–74 (*See also* interview techniques)

mining interviews for (*See* interview analysis)

sharing with sales departments, 173–175

C

Capabilities List, messaging strategy and, 140–147, *148–149*

Caterpillar, 159–160

causation, data correlation *versus,* 47

Cavett, David, 94

Challenger Sale, The, 176

challenger sales approach, 176–177

Chartered Institute of Marketing (CIM), 183–184

China, Beko sales in, 6–7, 160

C-level executives, campaigns to persuade, 30–34, 177–179

communication
about need for buyer personas, 28, 56–59

building Buyer Persona presentations, 123–128, *124, 125, 126, 127*

contact strategy for potential interviewees, 68–72

copywriting Buying Insights, 127–128

listening to customers/ interviewees and, xix–xxiv, 40, 81–82, 94–95 (*See also* interviews)

overcoming resistance to buyer personas, 55–59, 60, 186–188

communication (*continued*)
  to salespeople (*See* sales
    departments)
  with C-level executive buyers,
    30–34
  with other teams about buyer
    concerns, 193–194
competition
  choosing interviewees and,
    66–68
  competitive advantage and
    Buyer's perception, *91*,
    91–92
  interview questions about, 89
consent, to record interview,
    77–78
consideration, impact on buyer
    persona approach, 13–15,
    24 (*See also* high-
    consideration buying
    decisions, low-
    consideration buying
    decisions)
consumer appliance industry,
    6–7, 150
contact strategy, for potential
    interviewees, 68–72
content marketing
  messaging for (*See* messaging
    strategy)
  alignment with Buyer's
    Journey (*See* Buyer's
    Journey)

  strategy for (*See* Buying
    Insight, Buyer's Journey,
    messaging strategy,
    segmentation, solution
    marketing)
Content Marketing World
    Conference (2014), 153
continuous partial attention
    (CPA), 135
Cooper, Alan, 20–23, 190
copywriting
  brevity of, 164
  Buying Insights, 127–128
  educating Buyers with,
    163–164
  messaging strategy, 139, 150
Corporate Executive Board
    (CEB), 5, 176
cultural factors, understanding,
    3–4, 6–7, 114–117,
    160–162

D
"day in the life," of buyers, 24
Decision Criteria (Buying
    Insight 5)
  analyzing, by type of buyer,
    120
  defined, 27
  example of, *126*
  goal setting and, 187
  interview analysis for,
    100–110

messaging strategy and,
142–147, *148–149*
(*See also* Buying Insights,
Buyer's Journey, decision
making by buyers,
interviews, interviewing
techniques)
decision making by buyers
Buyer Profiles and, 7–10, *8*,
11–12
Buying Insights for, 12–13
high-consideration and low-
consideration decisions,
13–15
identifying decision makers for
interviews, 64–66
"know your customer" rule
and, 5–6, 57–59
market research importance
for, 3–7
reliance on demographics/
psychographics, 7–10, *8*
understanding, 7–10, *8*
demographics
finding interviewees and,
63–64
over-reliance on, 10, 12
segmentation and, 113–114,
118, *119*
DiMercurio, Dusty,
164–170
"discussion guide," for
interviews, 40

E
economic buyers, 64–66
educating buyers, 163–164
Eisenberg, Bryan, 41
Eisenberg, Jeffrey, 41
email, to request interview, 69
entering new markets, 114–117,
196–198
Everyone Writes (Handley), 150
Excel (Microsoft), for "Insights
Aggregator," 103–105, *104*,
105
expectations, of buyers, 23–25
(*See also* messaging strategy)

F
Facebook, 46
5 Rings of Buying Insight, 25–31
Buyer's Journey (Buying
Insight 4), overview, 26–27,
50, 101 (*See also* Buyer's
Journey (Buying Insight 4))
Decision Criteria (Buying
Insight 5), 27, 100–103,
105, *107*, *108*, *109*, *120*
(*See also* Decision Criteria)
determining number of
Buyer Personas needed,
115–117 (*See also*
segmentation)
including buyers in marketing
decisions with, 27–34
interview techniques and, 83

5 Rings of Buying Insight
    (*continued*)
  Perceived Barriers (Buying
    Insight 3), 26, 100, *126*, 141
    (*See also* Perceived Barriers)
  Priority Initiative (Buying
    Insight 1), 25, 79, 98, 100,
    101, 106, *119*, *125*, 151–
    152 (*See also* Priority
    Initiative)
  reviewing with internal
    stakeholders, 115–117
  Success Factors (Buying
    Insight 2), 25–26, 100,
    101–103, *125*, 142 (*See also*
    Success Factors)
  two Buyer Personas *versus* one
    Buyer Persona, 118–123,
    119, *120*, *121*
focus groups, 44–45
Forbes, 4

G
Geneen, Harol, 131
global perspective,
    understanding, 3–4, 6–7,
    160–162
goal setting, 185–198
  alignment and, 131–134
  Buyer Personas for strategic
    planning and, 194–198
  communication across teams
    for, 193–194
  for interview analysis, 97–98
  "marketing credibility" and,
    188–190
  potential and, 198
  product strategy and, 190–
    191, 192–193
  starting Buyer Persona
    initiative and, 186–188
Google searches, optimizing, 158
"group think," 45

H
Halvorson, Kristina, 153
Handley, Ann, 150
"headlines," for Key Insights,
    106–110, *107*, *108*, *109*, 117
high-consideration buying
    decisions
  defined, xxii–xxiii, 13–15, 24
  pricing models and
    perceptions of value, 29–30
  which buyers to interview,
    88–89 (*See also* internal
    stakeholders, interviews,
    interview analysis, and
    interview recruiting)
"high detail" persona," 159
how many buyer personas are
    needed, 111–122

I
incentives, offered to
    interviewees, 63, 68

industry marketing, 158–160

Inmates Are Running the Asylum, The (Cooper), 22–23

insight, 19–34 (*See also* Buying Insight)

internal stakeholders
  mock interviews and, 58–59, 60
  overcoming resistance of, 55–59
  overcoming resistance of, for setting goals, 186–188
  reviewing 5 Rings of Buying Insight with, 115–117

interview analysis, 97–110
  goals of, 97–98
  "headlines" for each Key Insight, 106–110, *107, 108, 109,* 117
  "Insights Aggregator" for, 103–105, *104, 105*
  interview transcripts for, 99–103, *100*
  number of interviews and, 98–99

interviewee recruiting, 55–72
  choosing which buyers to interview, 64–68
  finding time for, 59–60
  internal sources, 60–62
  professional recruiters, 62–64
  requesting interviews, 68–72, 77–78

resistance by internal stakeholders, 55–59

interviews
  as qualitative research, 39–41
  buyers' decision making and, 15–17
  conducting (*See* interview techniques)
  finding interviewees (*See* interviewee recruiting)
  for changes in buyer personas, 189–190
  importance of, 36–39, 51–53
  interviewer preparation for, 76
  mining for insight (*See* interview analysis)
  new products and markets, 196–198
  number of interviews needed, 98–99
  one-on-one, xxi–xxii
  testing segmentation options and, 114–117
  who should conduct, 51–52, 74–75

interview techniques, 73–95
  example of interview, 84–86
  gaining insight with, 73–74
  identifying interviewer, 74–75
  listening to answers, 81–82, 94–95
  note-taking during interview, 76, 80, 81

interview techniques (*continued*)
  preparing for interview, 75–77
  proficiency for, 98
  questions for interviews,
     78–94, *87*, *91*, *93*
  recording interviews, 77–78
iPhone (Apple), 3–4, 5–6, 160
iWatch (Apple), 192–193

J
Japan, iPhone marketing in, 3–4,
     5–6, 160
jargon interview responses,
     probing, 86–88, *87*
"Jessica" (Buyer Profile), 11–12
Jobs, Steve, 4, 195
journalists
  as interviewers, 74–75
  as marketers, 168

K
"Kathy" (user persona), 20–22
Key Insights, interview analysis
     for, 97–110, *107*, *108*, *109*,
     117. *See also* Buying Insight
"know your customer" rule
  defined, 5–6
  overcoming objections to,
     57–59

L
leads, generating, 28–29 (*See also*
     messaging strategy, Buyer's

Journey, solution
     marketing)
Line//Shape//Space, 167–170
LinkedIn, 49, 75
listening
  importance of, xix–xxiv, 40
  during interview, 81–82,
     94–95
low-consideration decisions
  as impulsive, 13–15
  understanding, 41–42
  (*See also* high-consideration
     decisions)

M
Macintosh (Apple), 22
Mangialardo, Donato, 190–192
marketing departments
  alignment with sales
     departments, 29, 60–62,
     131–134, 171–184 (*See also*
     sales departments)
  capacity of, 116
  vision for, 185–186, 188–190,
     194–198
Marketing Leadership Council
     (Corporate Executive
     Board), 5
marketing strategy, 131–164,
     188–189, 194–197 (*See also*
     Buyer's Journey, educating
     buyers, new products and
     markets, messaging strategy)

market research, 35–53
  big data for, 45–48
  buyer surveys for, 43–44
  finding time for, 59–60 (*See also* interviewee recruiting)
  focus groups for, 44–45
  importance of, 3–7 (*See also* Buyer Personas; decision making by buyers; interviews)
  investing in, 38–39, 116–117
  need for, 35–36
  qualitative research for, 39–41
  salespeople for, 42–43
  satisfying customer needs and, 36–38
  social media for, 48–49
  Web analytics for, 49–50, 158
  See also Buyer Personas; Buyer's Journey (Buying Insight 4); Buying Insight; interview analysis; interviewee recruiting; interviews; interview techniques
McKenna, Regis, 36–38
messaging strategy, 135–150
  alignment and, 131–134
  Buyer's Expectations and, 140–141
  Capabilities List for, 140–147, *148–149*
continuous partial attention (CPA), 135
copywriting, 127–128, 139, 150, 163–164
  effectiveness of, 28 (*See also* communication)
  evaluating competition for, 143–145
  pre-meeting contributions for, 139–140
  strategy workshop attendees, 138–139, 142–143
  traditional approaches, 136–138
Microsoft
  Excel, for "Insights Aggregator," 103–105, *104, 105*
  Powerpoint, for Buyer Persona presentation, 123–128, *124, 125, 126, 127*
"missing features," interview questions about, 92–94, *93*
mock interviews, with internal stakeholders, 58–60
moderator, for messaging strategy team, 138–139, 142–143

N
new products and markets, building personas for, 196–198

O

Ogilvy, David, 38

onboarding, 45–48

P

Perceived Barriers (Buying
   Insight 3)
   case study use of, 31–34
   defined, 26
   example, *126*
   interview analysis for, 100,
      101–110
   messaging strategy and, 141,
      147, *149*, 163–164
   sales enablement and, 177,
      193–194
   (*See also* Buying Insights,
      decision making by buyers,
      interviews, interviewing
      techniques)

permission, to record interview,
   77–78

persuasion, of internal
   stakeholders, 55–59, 60,
   186–188

phone calls, for interview
   recruiting, 69–72

playbooks, sales, 175

Powerpoint (Microsoft), for
   Buyer Persona presentation,
   123–128, *124*, *125*, *126*,
   127

pricing models, 29–30

Priority Initiative (Buying
   Insight 1)
   analyzing, by type of buyer,
      119
   Buyer's Journey and, 151–152
   defined, 25
   interview analysis for, 25, 98,
      100, 101–110
   messaging strategy and, 142–
      147, *148–149*
   understanding, 79
   (*See also* Buying Insights,
      decision making by buyers,
      interviews, interviewing
      techniques)

product demonstrations,
   interview questions about,
   89

product lifecycle management
   (PLM) software, 190–191

professional recruiters for
   interview scheduling,
   62–64

psychographics
   over-reliance on, 10
   segmentation and, 113–114

"pulling the thread," 82–84

Q

qualitative research, defined,
   39–41

"qualitative research recruiters."
   See professional recruiters

questions for interviews
about buyers' decision making
process, 88–90
about "missing features,"
92–94, *93*
about perceived competitive
advantage, *91*, 91–92
example interview, 84–86
to keep conversation flowing,
82–84
"open-ended," 91
pacing, 81–82, 94–95
probing jargon responses,
86–88, *87*
probing with buyer's words,
80
scripted opening question,
78–80
See also interview techniques

R
recording, of interviews, 77–78
recruiting interviewees. *See*
interviewee recruiting
Regis McKenna (marketing
and public relations firm),
36–38
*Regis Touch: Millions Dollar Advice
from America's Top Marketing
Consultant, The* (McKenna),
36–38
reorganization, problems of,
171–173

"results-oriented persona,"
159–160
Ross, Maribeth, 31

S
Sagent Technologies, 22
sales departments, 171–184
alignment with marketing
departments, 29, 60–62,
131–134, 171–184
as a source of buyer persona
insights, 42–43
buyer personas shared with,
173–175
challenger sales approach,
176–177
C-suite access by, 177–179
for finding interviewees,
60–62
marketing synergy, example,
179–183
marketing synergy,
importance, 171–173,
183–184
salespeople as interviewers,
74–75
sales playbooks, 175
sales prospects, as interviewees,
66–68, 75–77
SAP, 50
Scott, David Meerman, 6–7
screener for third-party
recruiting, 63

search engine optimization
(SEO), 158
segmentation, 111–130
building Buyer Profile,
128–129
Buying Insight and, 112–114
copywriting Buying Insights,
127–128
finding Buyer Profile
information, 129–130
goal of, 111–112
presenting Buyer Persona,
123–128, *124, 125, 126,
127*
testing options for, with
additional interviews,
114–117
two Buyer Personas *versus* one
Buyer Persona, 118–123,
119, 120, 121
silence, during interview, 94–95
smartphones
iPhone marketing in Japan,
3–4, 5–6, 160
measuring emotions with, 46
social media
developing content for, 139
as a source of buyer persona
insights, 48–49, 130
solution marketing
Buyer Personas used for,
158–160
prioritizing assets for, 156–157

See also 5 Rings of Buying
Insight
stakeholders, internal. *See*
internal stakeholders
Staresinic, Dan, 132
Stone, Linda, 135
strategic planning, 131–164,
188–189, 194–197
Success Factors (Buying
Insight 2)
as part of Buyer's Journey,
156–157
defined, 25–26
interview analysis for, 100,
101–110
messaging strategy and,
142–147, *148–149*
(*See also* Buying Insights,
decision making by buyers,
interviews, interviewing
techniques)
surveys, 43–44, 129, 162

T
"take me back to the day . . ."
(scripted interview
question), 78–80
targeted advertising, 47–48
team composition for messaging
development, 138–139,
142–143
technical buyers, 65–66
time issues

finding time to recruit
interviewees, 59–60
interview length, 69
transcripts, of interviews,
99–103, *100*

U
user personas, 23–24, 190–191

V
voice mail, leaving recruiting
messages on, 69–72

W
Web analytics, 49–50, 158
website experience, interviewing
buyers about, 82–83, 85–
86, 88, 95
website for content marketing,
164–170, (*See also*
messaging strategies)

Y
Youtility (Baer), 151–152